This book is to be returned on or before
the last date stamped below.

24 FEB 2000	13 NOV 2001	23 JUL 2002
25 APR 2000	11 DEC 2001	
01 AUG 2000	08 FEB 2002	27 SEP 2002
09 AUG	*Mr Mark* *MR*	12 OCT 2002
25 NOV 2000	20 MAR 2002	
25 APR 2001	17 APR 2002	27 OCT 2009 *14TH NOU*
24 MAY 2001	18 JUN 2002	12 APR 2013
	28 JUN 2002	

LEARNING FOR LIFE

RENEWALS   Please quote: date of return, your ticket number
and computer label number for each item.

A YEAR IN THE COUNTRY

A YEAR IN THE COUNTRY

by

Alison Uttley

Illustrated by
C. F. Tunnicliffe

HOWARD BAKER
LONDON

A YEAR IN THE COUNTRY

Alison Uttley

© Copyright: Alison Uttley, 1976

First published in the United Kingdom by
Faber & Faber Ltd., 1957

First published in this edition by
Howard Baker Press Ltd., 1976

ISBN: 0 7030 0100 0

WAL

A HOWARD BAKER BOOK

Published by Howard Baker Press Ltd,
27a Arterberry Road, Wimbledon, London S.W.20
Printed in Great Britain by Butler & Tanner Ltd,
Frome and London

CONTENTS

CONTENTS

All the months of the year,
Curse a fair Februeer

DECEMBER

Grey light lies on the hills, where rock and grass are the same hue, and the bare trees stand waiting, strong, malignant, held by their long thin roots from hurling themselves on their enemies. Winter has come, and a veil is pulled over to cover the earth itself, to conceal its real doings. At night, a frosty sky and glittering stars, an implacable dome above our small defenceless houses; a barking fox and a hooting owl call defiance. Footsteps ring on the hard ground, and voices carry through the still air. Doors are shut to keep out the cold and to protect the house from those beings which wander in the winter solstice even to the doors of Holy Church, seeking a home.

This is December, my own month, which binds its children with invisible cords of love to the time of frost and snow. St. Teresa of Avila explained her adoration of snow from her birth

9

DECEMBER

in winter, with snow as her first impression of a new world, and I humbly share this strong force of attraction which has always tugged at my heart, as soon as December dawns, bringing ecstatic contemplation of sky and air, where snow waits to fall. A great snowstorm swept the country, and no doctor could come through the drifts in the narrow roads which cut us off from neighbours, so the midwife, an old countrywoman in full gathered skirts, who smoked a pipe, delivered me safely in mid-December. She had been staying at the farm a week or two before my birth, as was the custom for these country nursing-women, when doctors were rare and their ways unpredictable. I opened my eyes to a first vision of white hills and fields around us. Surely this first sight of the living world must have an influence on a child; and when each birthday came round, my mother talked of that snowy day and I felt I belonged to the snow, as much as a snow princess.

In winter, up in the hill country, one is acutely aware of the earth spinning on its axis, rushing through space, the sole thing in motion which can be perceived. It is a ship, with stars in its rigging, plunging through the seas of ether or energy or whatever imponderable matter fills the vacancy, carrying its freight of humanity and its cargo of the invisible, solid mankind and thin ghosts, all swept onward towards Vega. So in December, the earth rides; while the moon on high changes her apparent pace, keeping company with the foot-traveller, or speeding to the uttermost spaces.

It seems fitting that a year not-quite-in-the-country but poised on the verge, pushed slightly away from the woods and fields, but retaining their company, should begin with December, the most evocative and mysterious of months. December is packed with emotions, with extra work compressed into minutes and timeless leisure stretching to eternity, with a feeling of urgency to prepare for Christmas, and a deep sense of ever-lasting peace, with contradictions all through its thirty-one days. It needs the full number to squeeze everything in the hamper of delights.

DECEMBER

In Buckinghamshire the snows of winter come later and although snow covers the hills of the Peak district and Yorkshire in the northern parts of the country, here it is often mild until Christmas is past. The earth is hushed, listening, expectant, it awaits the signal that the armies of wind and snow will attack, but the forces lie in ambush, gathering strength. There is a lull in the wild days about the twentieth and a mild spell lasts until the end of the month. Five days before Christmas, five days after, make this legendary interval, a holy space taken out of winter for the birth of Our Lord. Even when snow has come and the presages are for bad weather, there is often this quiet and peaceful interval of immortal time. The sky is golden blue at night, the earth is golden brown by day, and a curtain is drawn aside for the story of the Nativity to be played in all its beauty.

WINTER NIGHTS

Last night, early in the month, the sky was banded with crimson, with gold and rose streamers, and the first star shone through this frosty pageant. All the little boys who live near my house suddenly went mad with excitement. They shouted and yelled; they fired toy pistols and chased one another up and down the road. Cowboys and Indians running amok. In reality it was the clean icy life-giving December air that had gone to their hearts and wakened them—but I hurried out to cover my tender plants with cloches against the frost.

So, in childhood, we ran wild in the first days of December, as we flew with outstretched arms like wings, down the steep slopes of the hills, towards the sunset facing us in the western gap between two hills. The wind, far fiercer and colder than it is in this southern county, swept through our bodies, in spite of scarlet tam-o'-shanter, and scarlet scarves. This twilight play, with voices piercing and shrill, was part of winter, it was a gesture of defiance to the great powers threatening us in the days to come, when the wind might knock us down and uproot the great trees in its fury.

DECEMBER

We raced to the milking, to the cowhouses where the lanterns were lighted, a soft yellow glow which we could see from afar. As we hurriedly pushed a finger through the round hole to lift the latch on the inside, we were assailed by the life we loved, the only life we knew: the warm smell of cattle, and hay and linseed cake, the tinkle of milk falling in the shining cans, and the whistle and low song of the milkers. We shut the door behind us, and stood in the warmth, in the dim light, transported to a primitive world, the world of the Birth of Christ, with cows and warm breath and sweet hay. We drank the frothing milk in the china mugs we held out to our father to be filled from the cow's teats, we laughed at our white moustaches, and we told the latest news of sky and owls and foxes. We were answered in quiet monosyllables from my father, in rhythmic chewing from the cows, and shuffles in the straw. Then off we went, closing the door gently, making little noise, for cows do not like loud noises, and we dare not break the tranquillity of the cowhouses.

Across the wide field we could see the lamplight from the kitchen window, beckoning to us, a lighthouse in the darkness of the sea of grass and woods. We were alone in the world, with the great blue vault of the stars overhead and the woods and hills touching the sky, but we were safe, for there was home. We skipped across the field path, pausing only to get through the narrow stone stile that divided lawn from field. Is that art of skipping forgotten now? I seldom see children take that dancing step, with one foot raised, but it was our mode of progression when we were carefree. We never used the skipping step when we were sad, or in disgrace, or even when we were defiant.

The little town boys see the lights from their own windows only a few yards away, with no wolf- or fox-haunted field between, and no vast woods on their doorsteps with perhaps bears prowling, but they fire their brightly-gleaming large 'guns' and imagine they are on the prairies, as we fired our little black pistols with their penny boxes of scarlet caps. Perhaps they think a fierce animal is lurking in the shadows of the privet hedges, and an Indian lies in the laurel bush. A little six-year-old

12

DECEMBER

London child wrote his first essay for his teacher, for me to see.

'Once upon a time I saw in a wood a great big bear. He bit me. I ran home.'

So bears and wolves still haunt the woods of England, and this is as it should be.

AZALEAS

Today I have been to the little greengrocer's shop to buy azaleas and cyclamen for Christmas. I stood in the small country shop at a corner of the Old Town, choosing between flame and rose-coloured azaleas, and pink and petunia cyclamen. The window full of plants lighted up the shed-like place with its sacks of potatoes, its piles of grape-fruit and oranges. This strong-smelling earthy room, with a rival shop at the opposite corner, keeps its country atmosphere, although the town has grown so much, and I enjoy doing my shopping at one or the other of this pair of tiny booths.

These winter flowers are so entrancing, so luxurious, although they are inexpensive, that one is caught in the web of colour, in the richness and rarity they assume. I bought a very small azalea with white flecks on its frilled peach petals, and two cyclamen, rose-pink and purple-petunia. They belong to another world, a land of brilliance and fairytale, which Bluebeard's wife, Fatima, found before she saw the fatal key; where Cinderella strayed before she lost her glass slipper; where Beauty lived in the palace of the Beast. Cyclamens are birds with dipping beaks and arched necks, they are ballet girls in delicate skirts; they might fly clean away, they might sing or dance. Azaleas are roses of enchantment. I knew them in childhood, when they brought an air of romance and wonder which they still evoke with their ruffled petals.

Long ago, in my school days, a middle-aged bachelor, rich by our standards, courtly and kind, from an old family we had always known, came to stay with us for nearly a year while his ancient house was modernised and partly rebuilt. He had a sitting-room to himself; there he dined and breakfasted alone, and read the most exciting books which he bought lavishly. After he had gone to his office I dipped into these books, all new and beautiful. I read his magazines, the *Geographical Magazine* and *Blackwell's* and *Chamber's Journal*. He introduced me to Joseph Conrad's *Youth*, and in it he gave me my first taste of modern good writing, a change from the old-fashioned Dickens and George Eliot and Scott. He lent me a book by Ambrose Bierce, *In the midst of Life*, with short stories of ghosts and uncanny happenings which I implicitly believed. I trembled over them every night, I was haunted by them for years, although I never confessed my terrors. Conrad was a revelation of the power of language and I read each book several times, completely absorbed and lost in those tales of the sea.

He made us acquainted with flowers we did not know, azaleas, cyclamen, cinerarias, great golden lilies, King Alfred daffodils and blue hyacinths, growing in vast flower-pots which arrived each week. They were from the greenhouses of his home beyond the woods, and as the house was empty the under-gardener brought plants through the woods every Friday or Saturday to deck our plain rooms. In December and January came the azaleas, large bushes with dozens of blooms, with rose-shaped flowers, pink, snowy-white, and sealing-wax red, and twisty thick trunks like small trees.

They were to please my mother, and as she adored flowers we had these trees of enchantment on the floors, in the hall, and in his sitting-room and in the kitchen and parlour. We had never seen anything like them, for even the Squire had no azaleas as large as these. The 'roses' glowed in the candlelight and firelight of the house, and our friend liked candles and simple things around him, such as we had. Their petals were almost transparent, they were lights shining in the shadowy rooms. Their beauty affected me profoundly, I felt as if I were living in a fairytale of wonder, with magical trees, for I had never seen flowers in bloom at Christmas; we knew nothing of bulbs and forcing of flowers.

DECEMBER

Snow outside on the hills around us, snow powdering the lawn and stone walls and mighty trees, and these golden azaleas indoors! I came home from school by train at night, arriving in the milk cart with the servant boy driving and a load of empty milk-churns and my bag of school books, and I knew as we drove up the steep hills between the walls under the cold starry skies, with the cart lamps shining on the bare fields, I knew there would be this wonder of flowers in the house, perhaps even a new plant. I felt rich, enchanted, immortal, enshrouded with Beauty itself, beyond this life, although I was cold, tired and hungry. It was the wintry starlit sky under which I rode, it was the poetry of Jessica, of Rosalind, it was the music of Chopin, and the breath-taking prose of Conrad's *Youth*.

So azaleas bring this evocation of youth to me, because they were the first winter flowers I had seen. They were in the same category as the golden pheasant and his demure brown wife, which this benefactor of childhood gave to my father, a part of the outside world, of foreign lands. The cyclamen with their arched necks like swans, their sharp beaks and twisted feathers, were birds from Persia, pink and mauve and snowy white, dipping their demure heads to the earth, and books on Persia with golden pictures were on the sideboard, with these flowers.

Winter Berries

Azaleas and cyclamen are luxury flowers, but one cannot live on cake, and I go out to the woods and fields to find the bread of life, the common hedgerow berries and leaves which are the staple decoration for Christmas. Through the cherry orchards whose great trees are decayed, with holes in the trunks from which we poke brown dust, deep cupboards where birds roost at night, we go to the stile and the beech woods. It is a familiar place, where we seldom meet anyone. The tall bare trunks of the trees, like pillars holding up the lacy roof of branches, the blue haze between, the narrow track of grass and vivid moss, half hidden under the old brown leaves, with ivy and twigs, make a domain which I like to visit. The beech woods are deserted, and I miss the rustle of rabbits, and the sudden cry of pheasants and the company of small animals, red squirrels and stoats I used to find in my youthful days in woods, but my Scottie, Macduff, rootles in the leaves and squeaks with joy as he disturbs mice and hedgehogs.

A gale is blowing, for there is news of snow in Wales and in the north, and tempest round the coast. I was not aware of the strength of the wind today until I entered this kingdom of trees which catch the wind in their high boughs. The tree tops clash, they rock and sway together, and the sound of them is like the roaring of the sea on a rocky coast. It is like Tintagel in a storm, with the waves rushing into the caves, booming and roaring and beating on the cliffs. We walk into the wood, and the trunks are immobile, while the upper branches swing several yards in their amplitude, beating each other with clashing blows, sending their own waves of motion through the woods. There is a loud singing and sighing in the air, of which I heard nothing as I came across the wide cherry orchards. It is as if the wind lives in these woods.

We go through part of the woods, and then leave the trees for a narrow path between wood and ploughland, for here grows the ivy in great ivy-tods, green as emerald, striped with warm brown, tinged with white, veined with amber and crimson, ivy of many colours and shapes, smooth, long and angular, deeply notched like ferns, or even and regular. This wealth of ivy in Buckinghamshire intrigues me, it is so varied, so full of colour and glitter, unlike the green ivy of my youth. The soil must be responsible for the crimson and gold flecks in the wild little leaves, but our iron-water soil never produced such a wealth of colour and shape.

Traveller's-joy decks the hedges with cream feathers against the blue windy sky, and I gather some trails for Christmas. Red rose-hips shine and the hazels already bear small catkins tight as string on the twigs. We pick a bunch of this country wealth, choosing every kind of ivy, long trails and wreaths and top-knots, and sprays of rose-hips and firm twists of hazel, for the catkins will come out in water. Unconsciously I camouflage every piece that is broken off so that there are no marks on the bushes to show I have been there. So we were taught when we were small to hide our tracks, to smooth out the grass, to raise the ferns, to remove the tell-tale strip of white in the green branch so that no one following would see the bushes had been held aside to view the birds' nests, the flowers that had been picked. Like Red Indians, whose lives we studied on every occasion, we obliterated our trail. So the good habit has remained, the white sliver of twig is concealed with green rind, and hedge hides from boy or cat or marauder the hidden secrets.

We fill the bowls of copper and brass with the brightly gleaming berries and leaves, which seem to fall naturally and gracefully into shape, and we add the cork-coloured fronds of bracken and the sprays of yellow jasmine which is already in bloom on the house. I do not attempt the modern flower decorations with white-washed leaves and silvered edges, but sometimes after a sharp frost I bring in the cart-wheels of the giant hemlock, the 'kexies' of our childhood and of Elizabethan days, which Jack Frost, that arch-decorator, has painted with silver rime, furred and glistening. Frosted branches last a long time in my cold house, which has patches of warmth near the fires and cold icy corners. The kexies, and the silver-coloured seed heads of the great knapweed, called 'paint-boxes', and the tiny rose-hips like beads of sealing wax which cover an old-fashioned rosebush called Helenae, make a good December decoration.

A BUCKINGHAMSHIRE RECORD

A small paper-backed book has come today in cold December, and it gives me peculiar pleasure for it is the short history of a Buckinghamshire village written by two people who have lived all their lives in the place, whose roots are deep in country earth, whose memories go back to simple ways of living. The record has been compiled by them as a labour of love, a preservation of their local traditions, lest the village, like so many others, is swept into the grasp of a town. This seems unlikely at present, but they are taking no risks with an uncertain future when their country lore may be forgotten.

This small history of Stewkley is well-contrived, and the authors have used their intimate knowledge of life and work during the last seventy years, with links through the centuries. One of them, William Capp, a man of seventy-five, is a craftsman whose thatched cottage I visited some time ago to see the violins and violoncellos he had reconditioned and cured. He buys old broken instruments at village sales, and makes new parts, using the smooth white wood of box which grows on the Chilterns, and pine and pear wood; lengthening the tail-piece, making an inlay of box, and replacing the ivory tips of broken bows with the hard white box wood which resembles ivory. He is a clever joiner, and artist in his work, belonging to a family of joiners and carpenters.

Around the wall of the tiny cottage hung the instruments, seven of them, which he had mended and prepared for sale. In his youth he had been an amateur musician, a self-taught village fiddler, and he walked many miles at night after his day's work, with four friends who made up a string band for dancing in barns and parlours, and village inns. He started work at the age of ten, but when he was only eight years old he went 'crow-starving', as did many a little boy in the early years of life. One realises that the children got glimpses of wild life which they never forgot and the work was easy, but time went slowly for them. This child sat in a cornfield and waved a clacker when the crows descended on the ripe ears, to frighten the birds away. It was work the boys enjoyed, they were proud of earning money, although the day must have been eternally long. This small boy ate his dinner soon after breakfast, for an hour was a day to him.

An old friend of mine was a crow-starver in his childhood, and he told me he earned half-a-crown a week, a good wage. He was so efficient that the crows flew from his cornfield across the road, which is the main Oxford to London road, to the field opposite. The farmer there offered the boy three shillings and sixpence to starve the crows in his field, so he changed his employer and doubtless the crows flew back to his former field.

Did these children shout in shrill voices the traditional song of the crow-scarer?

> *Oh, all you little blackey tops,*
> *Pray don't you eat my father's crops,*
> *While I lay down to take my nap,*
> *Shuu-a. Shuu-a.*
>
> *If father he perchance should come,*
> *With his cocked hat and his long gun,*
> *Then you must fly and I must run,*
> *Shoo-oo-oo-a.*

The Cheshire song, sung in fields I know, is:

> *Bird away, bird away.*
> *Take a grain, leave a grain,*
> *And don't come here today.*

The boys were much more effective than scarecrows, and the swinging wooden clacker made a great din. I saw one in a country shop at Thame one day, when the market was busy and the farmers were there. I admired the ease with which one could swing it to scare the crows, but the noise was appalling. Three panels of wood are hinged together, and these clack loudly as the smooth much-worn handle is swept in a circle. I thought it might be useful to scare some of the noisy little human crows, but the sound of it might attract them, so I rejected it.

This little book gives a fascinating and true record of Buckinghamshire village life, brick-making, agriculture, joinery, artesian well-digging, brewing. The famous Stewkley beer was taken by waggons to Islington, to the White Horse Hotel, at the Cattle Market, for the drovers and dealers who liked this beverage. There was coachmaking, with sawyers, wheelwrights, coopers, making everything by hand with skill and pride.

DECEMBER

In the little slim book are some forgotten words, collected before they are altogether lost in education. 'Baver' is a snack of food, and 'Dewbit' a horseman's snack. 'Keach' is the verb 'to scoop', still used by country people here where women keach water from a stream, men take a baver with them when they go to work, and the water bubbling in the kettle is said to be 'quabbling'.

When their feet are wet they are 'wotchered', a fine old word for an unpleasant condition, and as they struggle home in rain and mud they say they are 'slummocking' home.

The word 'unkid' is used for strange, uncanny things, as in Shakespeare's day. It is Middle English for 'eerie', and it remains in this county where there are many 'unkid' spots, haunted by the unknown.

There is a reference to that ancient road, Steart Lane, a drover's road which crossed England. This drover's lane, which is part of the ancient cattle track from Wales to London, crosses in front of the village hall at Stewkley, and turns up Ivy Lane to the old 'Rose and Crown', where it turns left into the ford. Cattle have been brought along it from Banbury within living memory, say the writers of this little book. The oxen were shod at a forge in the village.

Parts of this very old track are known in many places, and once I was taken to a remote spot, a grass-covered lane with blackberry bushes and overhung hedges, winding through the fields near Quainton in Buckinghamshire. It was the haunt of gypsies, who had a camping ground on Steart Lane, and in the ditch stood a tombstone to a gypsy king.

Kilvert in his diary speaks of this drovers' road. 'Talking of Steart's Lane,' he said, 'it went to London. The continuation broke here but it could be traced all the way. It was recognisable at Swindon where it was called "The Old Lane to London". Cattle could be driven from Wiltshire and Gloucestershire to London in old days without paying toll.'

DECEMBER

ASH AND IVY

This is December 14th, a sunny day after rain, wind, and occasional frost, but this is a halcyon day. I went along my favourite lane, near the hamlet of Forty Green, a rough little road branching from the narrow high road which itself is but a one-way traffic road with passing places.

The banks of the lane are topped by hedges of slashed trees, which have not been trimmed this year, so the ash saplings are five or six feet long as they rise from the recumbent bodies of the ash trees, layered many years ago. These ash striplings are like the strings of a musical instrument, Pan's own harp, set in the air for the wind to play, and each string is a delicate pearly-grey against the afternoon sky. Each is tipped with its black bud, and little ears project on the smooth sweet stems, as if the harp-strings were listening. These ash branches are warm as flesh, smooth as skin, and their touch against my cheek is more human than the feeling of any other kind of tree.

The ash trunks, reclining, asleep, have small round cavities, moss-lined, fascinating as hiding places for wild life. The reason is not known to me, for no other tree has hollows quite as neat and entrancing as the ash. In childhood we used to put a finger inside, half-fearfully lest it should be nipped, as we tried to find something, an elf's scarlet shoe, a fairy cap, anything hidden by one of the secret people.

I picked some seed-boxes of a plant which was our childhood money, and I gathered some brilliant rose-hips and bright veridian mosses from the prostrate boles of the trees. Ivy, delicate, robust, strong and tender climbed on the banks, holding the soil from being washed away. The ivy leaves here are very small, and the web of the plant is a piece of green embroidery on the earth. Ivy is out of fashion, it is called Victorian, but it is Prehistoric, Saxon, it is Norman, Tudor and Stuart, with its everliving form and its mathematical angles. The ivy was used with holly for Christmas decorations in Tudor days, and there is an old song of the rivalry between the two, a carol of Henry VI.

DECEMBER

Holly he hath berries as red as any Rose
The foresters, the hunters, keep them from the does.
Ivy she hath berries as black as any Sloe
There came the Owls and eat them as they go.
Holly he hath birds, a full fair flock,
The nightingale, the popinjay, the gentle laverock.
Good Ivy, say to us, what birds hast thou?
None but the Owlet that cries: 'How, How?'.

We once gathered the ivy from the ivy bush, the great tod whose trunk was as thick as a man's thigh, and the berries, dark and flat, were dipped in sheep raddle to make them red, and into flour to make them white. Then these sprays of red and white berries were placed on a high shelf among the brass and copper vessels to be a sign of good cheer at Christmas, and we admired them as much as the holly, for their pointed leaves and shapes.

The nut trees in the lane have absurd little dumpy fingers held up to the wind, immature catkins, and a wisp of Traveller's Joy holds its grey beard and nods its hoary head at us. Over the hedge is the field, Old Dane, a rolling stretch which dips and rises to a wood and deserted orchard. Once a farm stood in this woodland, but nothing remains except the curled and twisted apple trees and cherry trees, where we go each year for blossom, and an old well. How long ago was it filled with life? A hundred years, an ancient man told me, but nobody knows. So back along the edge of Old Dane I walk with my moss and catkins and ivy sprays. The sun has gone down, the air is icy cold. It is winter, the shortest day is near, and snow is high in the air.

CHRISTMAS PREPARATIONS

A week before Christmas my mother and the servant girl and any helper we had staying with us, polished all the brass and copper in the kitchen and hall until it shone like gold. They beeswaxed the oak dresser and the chairs, the bureau and the grandfather clock, and cleaned and prepared the house as if they expected the king to visit us. Some of the herald angels might appear, flying down from the sky on great feathered wings, alighting on the lawn and viewing us.

The farm man and my father went to the woods with a rope and bill-hook to get holly. They brought back a load, carrying it on their backs, down the steep slopes of the pathless woods. It was stored in the brewhouse, for no holly or mistletoe must enter the house before Christmas Eve, or bad luck would follow. The mistletoe was cut the day before Christmas from a tall hawthorn belonging to a cottager, who was timorous of climbing. A little fir tree was dug in a plantation, to be returned when Christmas was over. All preparations of food and house and farm were ready.

So in this little house we have been house-cleaning for Christmas, although the house will be closed on the day, and every escutcheon and handle of bureau, chest of drawers and oak corner cupboard has had a bright polish, every brass candlestick and copper bowl is ready to hold its point of flame from the lighted candles. Sometimes my holly comes from the woods near, but it is difficult to find any in these days, and I buy it from a shop. Certain holly trees in the woods near have their berries reserved for the little church on the hill, and before Christmas young girls go out to cut the branches. Only twice have my own holly trees in the garden held berries, but there is bay, and rosemary, fir and ivy sprays in my own small wood, all ready for the decorations.

The ancient Christmas tree, an artificial tree which I bought many years ago in Cheshire, comes out each year, and although it is bedraggled, it has the same charm and lightness and gaiety as of old. With it in the oak chest are the glass balls and bells and silver doll's house, the glass bird, the stars and half moons, the paper Chinese lanterns, the long strings of silver balls, which also date back to the days of my country home. Some indeed belong to my childhood, but they are faded, and not as pretty as the spun glass toys. Some of them have a tiny coloured picture attached, one of those 'scraps' which were so popular in late Victorian days.

DECEMBER

Now the little tree on the piano winks and blinks with its silver-gilt balls, its gold and blue bells tinkle their glass clappers, as they swing in the draught from the open window, and the silver bird with its long spun-glass tail shakes a feather for it remembers the two score years it has silently sung its Christmas song on a Christmas tree, in an old farmhouse, then in a Cheshire house, and now in a small modern Buckinghamshire cottage. Nobody kisses under the mistletoe bough which hangs in the hall, for the custom of embracing everybody, old and young, rich and poor at Christmas, is lost; we are over-fastidious. Guests pass under it without a glance at the pearly berries. Only when the house is alone the inanimate things have their own way, kisses and beckoning fingers call to leaf and flower and feather. The unseen world has entered the house on Christmas Eve with the holly and the ivy and the mistletoe, the wood sylphs are here, enjoying their invasion of the world from which they were expelled by Christianity, or rather, by the Church, for Christianity embraces everything visible and invisible, snow, holly and robins, as it chants:

'O ye Ice and Snow, bless ye the Lord; praise him and magnify him for ever.
O all ye Green Things upon the Earth, bless ye the Lord; praise him and magnify him for ever.
O all ye Fowls of the Air, bless ye the Lord; praise him and magnify him for ever.'

Holly and ivy, bay leaves and silver fir, rosemary sprays and mistletoe are in the house together, and the scarlet holly over Flemish landscape and Dutch flower pictures signals to the fire, the ivy binds the bookcase with trailing leaves, the bay fills the spaces over the corner cupboards and oak dresser, among the old china dishes. Once we put a spray of holly with bright berries over every jug and dish-cover, and between all the Staffordshire plates on the dresser. I cannot find enough holly sprigs to continue this custom even if I had the time and the patience.

24

DECEMBER

The scent of the woods is strong, the fragrance of moss and leaves, of fir boughs and crushed rosemary comes from the decorations as one enters the room. It is companionable and good, the odour of the earth which we so often forget. In Church it overpowers even the perfume of the worshippers, it brings a far older and traditional smell which rises like the incense in Roman Catholic churches.

Always in the background at Christmas-time were the woods and fields, with their own secret life of which I was deeply aware. The naked trees now showing their forms, the stone walls, austere and living, the little paths, were all very much more in evidence. Like the shadows which ran about the house, climbing the stairway with the candles, sweeping like giants over the ceilings, so were the invisible shades that appeared at this time of the year. Winter is the time when the earth lives, and has power. Feet patter over the hills, wings fly in the winds, hair streams in the clouds. A bird calls with mournful but triumphal cry, as it soars over the woods. The owls wail and hoot, telling us something we cannot understand yet, for our knowledge is limited to a thin shell.

So in the past there was a deep contrast between the gay warm lighted interior and the bare fields that pressed around, and I looked through the unshuttered windows across the lawn and watched for the first star with apprehension and bliss. Fastening the shutters always had this effect upon me, but at Christmas there was an added intensity of emotion. To stand by a window, separated only by a sheet of glass from the wildness of nature was something that caught my heart. I lingered, staring through, and everything seemed to be waiting to be alone under the stars. Then, with pounding heart, because I thought I had discovered the secret of life, I dragged the shutters from the wall, unfolded them on their well-oiled hinges, and closed them over the glass. I lifted the long iron bar, and let it drop into the neat socket, compact as a key in a lock. Nature was left to her own devices out there.

DECEMBER

CHRISTMAS EVE

On this morning of Christmas Eve I have been to watch the bevy of decorators at work in the small ancient church to which I go. Some of them were hanging long garlands of holly in loops about the Jacobean pulpit, in the manner of Victorian days, and perhaps this is the prettiest way to adorn it. They tied up the loops with scarlet ribbons to match the berries, and the festive red was present in eight tall candles in the brass candelabra, high up between the arches over the choir. I always wonder how they manage to polish this intricate and beautiful piece of brass which was once discovered black with dirt and age in a corner. Is there a step-ladder long enough to reach it?

A Christmas tree stands in a side aisle with its tip brushing the lower roof. The vicar is superintending the lights and the red and blue balls which hang on its boughs. At the west end of the homely church is the model of the stable at Bethlehem, with its thatched roof, beautifully thatched like many a Buckinghamshire cottage with criss-cross laths making an edging. The Holy Family recline inside among hay and straw fresh from the farm across the road. Joseph, Mary and the Babe in the manger, the Ox and the Ass, safely held back behind two wooden bars, the shepherds kneeling, all are there in that eternal scene, with the bright star shining in the blue sky through the open door.

One of the most picturesque stories associated with the Nativity is that of the presence of the Ox and the Ass in the stable at the birth of Our Lord. There is no mention of the beasts of the earth in the New Testament, but the legend has persisted since the fourth century. In mediaeval pictures the animals are there, gazing at the scene. One could hardly suppose the stable was empty in a time when so many travellers were at the inn. Surely it was warm with the breath of animals, with straw on the ground and hay in the manger, a real dwelling place for the homeless, and cleaner and quieter than the overcrowded foul-smelling Eastern inn. The animals bring a domesticity to the home in the stable, a link which binds man and beast together at this transcendent moment. It is a simple country background to eternity invading time.

The dwelling places of animals have often been chosen as refuges and hiding places by fugitives and the homeless. They have been invaded by the very young and the very old, who feel near the animals in spirit. I remember an aged man who used to disappear and sit in a corner of the stable to read his paper. Boys went there to practise the mouth-organ or the home-made flute. We retreated there to sit on a three-legged stool to talk to the mare and watch the chaffinches in the doorway. In the stable was the everyday harness with bells and brasses hanging on the wall, and a striped yellow and red horse-rug, strong-smelling and bright as an Arab cloth. Curry-comb, brush and surcingle lay in the stone cupboard cut out of the wall's thickness. The flat stones of the floor, laid on the rock of earth itself, were covered with fresh straw where the horse stood, but swept bare for our feet. Time was not, and when we came out bewildered to another life, time's pendulum wagged again. To stand in the darkness with a lighted lantern on the floor was most bewildering and strangely exciting, a world cut off, with light and shadow like a Rembrandt interior.

In childhood I used to play with a little boy in a high old farm in the hills when my father went to visit the place. The parlour was built over a cowhouse, for the house was on a higher level than the farm buildings, and one walked down a flight of steps to the yard and water troughs. The parlour had a wooden floor instead of stone as in the other rooms, and we could hear the slow movements of the cattle below. When, grown older, I stayed there for a few days, I sat quietly in this room, while the family lived in the kitchen, and the sounds of the cows, the soft moo, the rattle of the iron chains, the snuffles and the restless movements of the heavy bodies, the sighs and the thud of cloven hooves were so close I was startled. It was a good sound, a familiar kindly noise, for the animals were well fed and I was happy to be near them, just overhead. It was a sharing of life with animals, and they doubtless liked to have human beings near them, for all domestic animals enjoy society and abhor loneliness.

Kilvert relates in his diary that he had dinner at 'The Old Inn', near Mullion Cove. The sitting-room was over the stable, and they heard the horses stamping underneath.

So we used to sit in the stable, or lean over the door, and we talked to the horses, we climbed to the ledge of the pig-cote to chatter to the piglings, and we discussed our affairs with the heedless hens, the Jersey cow, and the dog. We tried to get the feeling of the life of these others, there was no great barrier between man and animal, and no sentimentality in our relations; we saw the wisdom of some animals, we were aware of the sagacity and faithfulness of these creatures, beings in the world, not cut off from us. Childhood, when the senses are preternaturally acute, is aware of affinities which later are forgotten, but at Christmas these contacts with Nature are remembered.

CHRISTMAS

Christmas is over, and there is the sense of deep regret, a vain longing for it to last for ever. The end of holidays, the end of a concert, the fading of a sunset, always bring this feeling of the transitoriness of life, a chapter is finished.

I have spent the festival days in the north of the county. We drove through the little villages in the darkness of Christmas Eve, past Christmas trees alight in the small towns. Penn Church had a lighted yew tree in the churchyard, close to the great oak door, among the graves. Amersham's tree shone out bravely, and the arched Guildhall and the church with flood-lighting made a Christmas card scene unreal in its enchantment. At Aylesbury the tree stands in the market-place, and at Winslow there are two trees, one for the workhouse, one for the village. The air is icy cold as it blows across the flat Plain of Aylesbury, the villages are completely rural, for this is an agricultural land with many farms and much ploughland, with hedges well-plashed and villages self-contained and individual. There are no black-coated workers hurrying for trains, but one meets a man carrying a gun, a boy driving cows, a youth with a tractor, and everyone hails us familiarly.

The cottage is early seventeenth century, scarcely altered except for an added kitchen with all the electric amenities known to civilisation. Otherwise it is a simple country cottage with thatched roof and timbered walls and heavy old beams stretched across the ceilings, with sloping floors and ceilings which hit the unwary. The oak staircase winds inside a wall, rising abruptly from the sitting-room, through a door in the wall, twisting through two right angles with steep change of pitch and sloping slippery stairs. We stumble and climb sometimes on hands and knees up the three-cornered stairs in this spiral way which leads directly into my bedroom.

At the back of the cottage fields spread down to the river. The front of the cottage is on a narrow lane, and cattle pass close to the windows, occasionally stopping to stare within, as they go to the farm across the road. The sound of their hooves slithering along the grass and cobbles wakes me in the morning, and I feel suddenly homesick, for it is a country noise I miss.

The cottage is decorated with yellow holly berries from Stowe Park, as well as red, with branches of lovely evergreens, with a kissing bunch and a little Christmas tree. We go to church early in the morning, in the soft cold light, past the farmhouse, and a fiddler sits in the aisle to help the music. We meet friends, we visit houses, and walk by the river down windy deserted lanes with the dogs.

On Christmas morning after church, we went into Stowe Church to see the decorations. It is a little church so secluded by trees that I had never before discovered it, although I had searched in the park. There is a fine tomb with the following inscription which is light-hearted as a cowslip ball. It is the tomb of Martha Penystone, born a Temple, and we stood there for a time imagining the lovely girl who once walked in the avenues and among the temples of Stowe.

DECEMBER

'Shut in this sepulchre lyes the ashes of Faire Penyston, who, lov'd by the most worthy of her time, removed to Heaven so to draw up hir lovers' eyes to the divine beautie of that deitie wherein she may love all that love hir and not sinne.'

The altar cloth, at Christmas, is one made from an embroidered wedding dress of somebody long-dead, and we remembered that often in Buckinghamshire churches we have found lovely bits of domestic embroidery finishing their lives in church.

We go to Buckingham where the golden swan swings in the wind on top of the Town Hall, a weather-vane, and we admire the fine Christmas tree which stands in the empty market-place. It was one of the first to be erected in a public place, and for years one of the townsmen has given this tree. It stands there, under the stars, with few lights and a vast space around it, so one can see the sky above. It appears to have reality, to grow there, an integral bit of Christmas, a poetical tree, different from all the made-up trees in other places.

We drive along the lonely roads, over the low mediaeval bridge, where sometimes I see swans, to a moated village with high walls and a narrow footbridge. In a small thatched cottage, a Hans Andersen cottage, lives an old lady who makes lace. She is a friend of mine, and I always visit her on Christmas Day to take a small gift. Today I walk up the narrow path, and tap at the door. There is no answer. She is out, paying her visits, so I unlatch the door and enter to leave my packet of chocolate and sweets on the table in the diminutive cottage of a ballet or fairy-tale, a cottage where people have worked and saved, lived and died for two hundred years. There is one room downstairs, with a fire burning in the shining grate, Christmas cards on the mantelpiece, a clock on the wall, and a red bobbed cloth on the table. Off this room is a slip of a room, like a cupboard, which holds the lace pillow, the bobbins, carved and fretted, of bone and of wood, and the lace patterns. I used to come here to watch the nimble fingers make the delicate Buckinghamshire lace, and to chat to my friend, who talks well, and tells many a tale of her girlhood in the village before she went to London in service.

DECEMBER

NORTH MARSTON CHURCH

On a bleak icy-cold morning at the end of the month, I drove along the narrow Buckinghamshire lanes in the north, to pay my devotions to a favourite church in the county, which I only see once a year. The ancient church of North Marston was once of such fame that pilgrims came from all over England to see the shrine which the church contained. In the chronicles it was mentioned as equal with Walsingham's holy place. Now I am a solitary pilgrim.

So we sped on the grey bitter day through the roads which thread the fields, roads which had recently been flooded by winter rain and villages cut off. We crossed a very narrow stone bridge only just above the water level, and I remembered a tale told to me by an old man who was born at North Marston. His father told him the tale of Neild, the wealthy antiquary, who left his fortune of £250,000 to Queen Victoria when he died in 1852. Neild, who was reputed to be a miser, used to save every penny, and he walked to Winslow or to Buckingham instead of taking the carrier's cart.

One day the rains fell, the roads were flooded and the little bridge which spans the stream was under water. The floods were very bad, and in the usual custom of those days, a villager stood by the bridge to carry people over for sixpence a time. Everybody willingly paid to be lifted across the water.

Mr. Neild arrived at the bridge, and he insisted that threepence was enough. So he was carried half-way and then dropped neatly into the water in the centre of the bridge.

'No further without thou payest another threepence,' said the Victorian St. Christopher. 'Half-price, half-way.' And old Neild had to pay, much to the satisfaction of the village people.

Just beyond this bridge is the church of Granborough, and I stayed a minute or two to look at the tiny alabaster group which was once dug up from the churchyard, broken but immortal in the exquisite carving of drapery of the women at the cross. The

31

little group hung in the chancel, beautiful as I remembered, but the church was colder than the grave and we hurried out to the warm air of the icy morning, for there are degrees in coldness and this was like the tomb itself.

North Marston church, warm, cared for and happy, seemed to be filled with life and busy invisible happenings. We might have interrupted them, and the quizzical carved heads nodded to one another, the ugly humorous faces squinted down, like workmen caught in the dinner hour playing cards in a holy place. For these heads, carved on the pillars and walls, are some of the most entrancing and spirited I know. They speak with mouths awry to conceal moving lips, they tell ribald jests, they remember the pilgrims of seven hundred years ago, and in those times there must have been many a queer tale to tell and sight to see.

The church is strangely alive; it is packed with memory and legend of Sir John Schorne, who was rector in the thirteenth century. He challenged the Evil One and pushed the Devil into a boot and kept him there. He worked miracles, but he was never canonised, perhaps because his miracles were unorthodox even in a miracle-working age. Statues and paintings represent him with his trophy, the boot, and crowds went on pilgrimage to his church.

On this day of December we went to see the decorations, the long trails of holly and ivy fastened round the Norman pillars, the little Christmas tree, very small and meagre as if it dare not hold up its green branches among those pagan ugly faces which sneered at the Victorian tree in the new Elizabethan era.

The expression of the faces was so cynical, so contemptuous, that one could almost hear the voices of the men.

'You and your atom bomb!' they seem to say. 'What did we tell you? There is nothing new. We are all alike, sons of Adam.'

We went to the chancel to find again a favourite sign. A carved stone hand and a long forefinger points down to the earth, and two crossed bones are near it.

DECEMBER

Here lieth the
body of Mr. John

Virgin, Ministerr
of North Marston.
who decesed this
life the 6 day of
January, 1694.
Aeged 77 years.

Then the dramatic words follow

He Lise Dust downe
thare.

After this warning sign we drove on, past Sir John's well, whose waters sprang up when he struck the earth, past the little dolls' house cottages by the side of the road, which were built on the road verge it is said, and up the long hill to Oving. We passed some round haystacks, with decorated top-knots and one of these was the lovely figure of a bird made of straw. It was well-cut and modelled, with smooth head and long tail. It was such a delight to see this yellow bird, probably a cock, against the sky that I felt grateful to the unknown thatcher who had made a thing of beauty for all who passed to admire.

JANUARY

New Year's Day is welcomed by good wishes. 'A Happy New Year' we say, almost automatically, but in our country houses the New Year was brought in by a dark stranger, who would carry good luck. So our servant boy with black hair was in request to knock at a door of a farmhouse a mile away, and to enter and receive a shilling.

Kilvert says: 'We always had a dark-haired man to bring in the New Year. He knocked and was bid enter. He came to the kitchen door. A new shilling was given to him. He brought good luck. This is the first-footing of the New Year.'

We waited up to hear the church bells ring in the valley, and then we danced outside the door, and knocked and entered, and we drank mulled possets, bread and milk, with spices, and wine or ale, according to one's taste. There were small presents, trifles, a pincushion, a ribbon, a handkerchief, and kisses, for it was the only night in the year when we sat up till midnight. On

JANUARY

New Year's morning we always had family prayers, a serious occasion, for prayers were for night-time. We had a New Year's dinner, with a roast pheasant and plum pudding, for this was an important day, carrying great power and influence through the year.

'If you cry on New Year's Day, you will cry all through the year,' said other children. We determined to be better, and for at least a day there was an improvement. At night we asked riddles, we played forfeits and turned the trencher, and acted charades—and we drank elderberry wine, mulled with cloves.

The custom of giving presents at the New Year is far older than that of Christmas present-giving. It dates from the Epiphany, the gifts of the Wise Men to the Holy Child. Lately I saw a list of gifts which Queen Elizabeth I received.

A Bible covered with cloth of gold, garnished with silver-gilt, from the Master of the Savoy; a box of foreign sweetmeats from the Queen's Physician; another physician gave a pot of green ginger and a pot of orange flowers; her apothecaries a box of lozenges and a box of ginger candy; Mrs. Blanch gave a little gold comfit box and a spoon; Mrs. Morgan a box of cherries and one of apricots; the Queen's Master Cook and Sergeant of the Pastry various confectionery and preserves; Putrino, an Italian, two pictures; Ambrose Lupo gave her a box of lute strings, and a glass of sweet water; each of three other Italians presented her with a pair of sweet gloves; a cutler gave her a meat knife having a fair haft of bone with a conceit in it; Jeremy Bassano gave two drinking glasses; and Smyth, the dustman, presented her with two bolts of cambric.

This is such a charming homely list, of small and excellent gifts; it might do for a modern household. Sweets and preserves, lozenges and gloves, a knife and glasses. Times have not changed very much.

THE KALENDS

In January the days begin to draw out we tell each other hopefully, so we look at the clock and regard the sky and make comparisons of darkness and light, and we find that the daylight is really a few seconds longer. We are surprised; it is an extraordinary fact, we almost feel as if we had had something to do with this miracle because we made the prophecy, but we remember the saying, 'As the day lengthens, so the cold strengthens.'

In Buckinghamshire the countryman uses an ancient bit of weather lore, which has often been quoted to me by labourers and hedgecutters.

> *If the Kalends of January be smiling and gay,*
> *You'll have wintry weather till the Kalends of May.*

It is good to hear the Roman word for the first three days of the month used by thatcher and hedger. Many people think the first three days of the year rule the first three months in weather, and are the presage of weather in September.

The moon is regarded closely at the beginning of the New Year, and Kilvert in his diary speaks of the moon as 'a very keen moon' when it was seen for the first time in the year. 'Old fashion folk used to take great notice of the first moon of the New Year,' he adds.

Long ago I discovered that winter is like tomorrow, it never comes. It threatens and swears and frowns, it drops its burden of snow, and then it displays its brown buds hidden on the beech boughs, and its green trails of honeysuckle in the woods. Today a touch of yellow in a corner of a field made me stoop to find a small buttercup, round and secure as a tiny gold nut, a word in season, a message of Spring perhaps, for the day was bitter, and the wind cut like a carving knife. There seemed to be no sign of anything but bad weather. I then saw a grove of green hellebores in a garden by the field, and the owner gave me a bunch to take home.

The Greeks throw a kiss to the sun as a welcome each day, and I do the same when I first see the gleam in the east, for the primitive and pagan act is a small token of worship, a salutation to the sun-god. We send a kiss after a chimney-sweep for luck, we still bow to the new moon, so why should the furtive sun not receive his welcome?

BIRD VISITORS

The robin sings before dawn, he is the first singer in my garden, where he tosses his notes away, and ripples and chants in delicious abandon in the semi-darkness. He is out on the lawn waiting near the french window for crumbs, calling to me if he sees me draw a curtain in the dim light. Then the sun comes up with long crimson streamers across the sky, and between the rose and the gold lies the blue of far heaven. After the robin's welcome, the blackbird and thrush appear, questing with sudden little runs, but never a note do they utter. The storm-cock sings in a high tree, and flocks of tits and finches are flying in the wood, chattering a good deal in company. Blackbirds are silent, but they visit the bird table and bathe in the stone trough. They stare through my window from the summit of the garage, a favourite place of inspection, and they flick the water from their feathers and leave a white streak of bird droppings down the roof in one spot only.

The starling in a chestnut tree whistles cheekily; but he is no friend of mine, and I refuse to be taken in by that clear fresh call. He bows his glittering head, and bobs in a companionship of four who take all they can, and snatch all the food I put for other birds.

The jays have been invisible for a long time, but I saw a pair of magpies bright as a black and white decoration, strut and play together on a neighbour's lawn. They come every day from the wood and later they will pair and build a nest in the high trees. Magpies always give me a new sense of astonishment. I can never get used to their beauty, although I have seen them all my life, and heard curses hurled down upon them. The combination of colour is spectacular. Friesians are my favourite cattle, a piebald pony is a delight. Black and white cats, zebras and antelopes, black and white pebbles, then blackthorn boughs with snowy flowers clustering upon them, all these are a pleasure. Once I saw the production of Twelfth Night in black and white, a theatrical venture which was as beautiful to the eye as to the ear. So the black and white magpies strut like actors on the stage, they fly to the trees and shake their long tails, sinister and malign beauties, whom I scare away when other birds are nesting.

A magpie sat on a cottage wall in the wildest part of Wales, very close to me, and for a moment I thought it was going to speak. It was like a familiar spirit, a changeling, and I have never forgotten that sudden impact of a bird's personality.

There is a magpie riddle which we asked one another:

> *As black as ink and isn't ink.*
> *As white as milk and isn't milk.*
> *As soft as silk and isn't silk.*
> *And hops about like a filly-foal.*

I am superstitious about magpies, and I feel a slight discomfort if I meet only one, but even this apprehension is mingled with delight in the bird. There is an old way of circumventing the bad-luck which follows the single pie, and it is to bow with extreme courtesy to him, and say in salutation: 'Good morning, sir,' or 'Good evening, sir'. A man who meets a magpie must take off his hat and speak to the bird. All this goes back to a close and intimate connection with nature, a friendship, a realisation of the life of others beside man.

Where does the tradition of bad luck come from? Perhaps from the knowledge that the birds suck eggs, and the magpies are always disliked round the poultry-yard. The game-keepers shot the jays and hung their bright bodies on an oak tree, for they stole the pheasant eggs from the hen coops in the woods when rearing was taking place, but I never once saw a magpie hanging up. It was unlucky in Derbyshire and Cheshire to kill a magpie, and cows might die at the farm.

JANUARY

Magpie, Magpie, flutter and flee,
Turn up your tail and good luck come to me

is another saying, for if it flirts its tail it accepts the companionship of man and brings him fortune.

The well-known rhyme for a company of magpies runs:

One for sorrow, two for joy,
Three for a girl and four for a boy,
Five for silver, six for gold,
Seven for a secret never to be told.

I have never seen more than four magpies at once, for in my country places they are not as common as blackberries, but we always look for a second bird to turn our sorrow to joy. A company of magpies is called a 'tidings', for perhaps to the simple country people they once brought news, strange and occult.

On January 3rd a green woodpecker came to my garden, and climbed an apple tree, pecking the crevices of the trunk. Usually the birds walk about on the lawn, probing the ground with their sharp beaks. When rain has soaked the grass they come, two or three at a time, they dip their heads with snaky grace, and eat and eat with swift pokes and quick movements, looking towards the house between the stabs in the soil. We have to be very still lest they see any movement through the windows and fly away. I creep about the room and stand in the shadows for they hear every sound. Often they come very near, and no work is done while they are in the garden, for they are beautiful creatures and I am honoured by their presence.

The great green woodpecker is called a whetile in Buckinghamshire, or a rain-bird, and it has the reputation of foretelling rain with its call. Later in the spring the laugh rings in the woods, and yaffle or yaffingale is a country name. In January they are silent and I see very few as early as this.

Coal-tits, great-tits, long-tailed tits, and tomtits are here every day, swinging on the coconut, playing around the bird table.

JANUARY

All this gay company makes a delight in the early month, so each morning there is the excitement of watching for new and old friends.

A flock of hawfinches invaded my garden on January 1st, on a morning of misty rain. They flew down from the wood and hopped about the grass, picking up the seeds of the hornbeam, biting them and cracking them so that I could hear the tiny sound of their curved beaks in the stillness. Sometimes the seeds filled their mouths so that their beaks would not shut, and they cracked and bit with vigour, shaking their heads violently. All the time they made a thin little song, a twitter of joy, a conversation with one another like a congregation of country folk who had come to explore the market. Last year, too, they came, these plump little birds with creamy beaks hooked like very tiny parrots. Their heads are bronze, on bluish necks, and stout little bodies. They are individuals. They feed like a flock of hens in a farmyard, intent and busy. Then, as if a private warning has been given, they fly away with a sudden swoop into the woods.

I am delighted to have them although I have to view the flock from a distance, for they never approach the house. When they arrive they spread out and quarter the ground, as if they had already arranged the division. I go out afterwards to examine the holes they have made with their beaks as they dig. They are the shyest of visitors, for even the jay and the magpie eat from the bird table, and the green woodpecker and spotted woodpecker come near the window.

I stood on a hilly field to watch a skylark rising on a late day of January. The bird rises almost vertically with its head to the wind and its wings beating deeply. It is a 'living organ', a marvel of music. My skylark sang for more than three minutes this January day when all was cold and still in winter's grip, but the sun was shining on the woods. The 'ceiling' reached is two or three hundred feet, but sometimes it is a thousand feet high. There the flight is in a small circle, and still the bird faces the wind. Down he drops, in a dive, singing all the time nearly to the ground. This bird sang with the utmost rapture, and I stood marvelling, longing to keep this particular song for ever. It was something out of eternity, beyond all time.

On January 8th I heard the first great-tit call with his bell-like voice, a welcome song. The missel thrush sings every day, and two blackbirds are courting each other under my window— or perhaps they are playing a game. They run with quick little steps, they pretend to peck each other, the male flirts with his tail, the lady bows, they carry on a delicious entertainment, oblivious of me.

The robin welcomes me each day as I draw my curtains downstairs. One robin enters the kitchen every morning, he loiters about at the back door until the door is left open when he enters and explores. It is not for food alone, he enjoys flying about to canister and to chairback, to coffee mill, to table. The jays are now squawking in the wood, flying over with hard eyes glancing at me, down to the bird table. They refuse to move even when I clap my hands. I shout 'Bang, bang', pretending to be a gun and they laugh.

Early this morning there was a hoar frost, which made every blade of grass like a sparkling knife. The beech trees were jewelled with the frost. Macduff rushed out and rolled his stout little black body on the frosty earth, to get the feeling of the crystals in his blood. Later when the snow was deep I played snowballs with him, and he tried to catch each snowball in his mouth, dancing and barking, begging me to throw all the great expanse of snow in a million balls for him to catch. So I took him to a field to watch the children on their toboggans. It was too exciting for him. He strained on the lead, wishing to dash after them.

FOXES

Foxes abound and one was seen in Padbury in full daylight the other day, loping quietly across the fields which were snow-covered so that he was distinctly visible, quite near us. The field spaniel, Gunner, chased him, a grand run over three broad fields, dog and fox running 'hell for leather', the dog eager, the fox care-free, for he knew he could get away.

A year or two ago a friend saw a col-fox or a brent-fox in these same fields. A col-fox is a dark variety, a brent-fox is very dark, almost black, a rare animal. Chaucer says: 'A col-fox full of sly iniquitie'. The name is a variant of cole-fox.

In the north of Buckinghamshire foxes are hunted by the Whaddon Chase and the Grafton Hunt, and shot by farmers. Seven came out of a cornfield in September when the wheat was cut, and of these four were shot and three escaped. If a fox is hit with a bullet it always dies, say the country people. Gangrene sets in and death follows. I would like to know if this is true.

It is always surprising to those who do not know foxes to realise how small is the animal and how red is his colour. Long ago I was strolling over our own fields in the north country, picking flowers, and a fox appeared near me. It took no notice of me and at first I thought it was a reddish dog. It ran slowly along the grass to the high wall, and then it went over in an astonishing manner with none of the leaping and clambering of a dog. It seemed to flow over the stones like a snake, a lovely sinuous animal, and on it went, across the field to another wall, and over that with such grace and ease I realised it was a daylight fox. Foxes are enemies, and we were never sentimental about them. No farmer was allowed to shoot a fox, and when one was 'accidentally shot', the fact was kept secret.

Foxes raided the henroosts of unfortunate neighbours, and there was a story of a raid on our own henhouse, when there was a great slaughter of hens. It seemed impossible that a fox could mount the narrow ladder against the high side of the building, and enter the narrow trapdoor weighted and fastened each night. This was in a January night when snow was on the ground. The marks of the fox pads could be seen and the animal was tracked down the long fields, across the road to the wild river's edge. In curiosity to find out where it went next, someone went along the road to the bridge a mile away and tracked back to the river's opposite bank. The fox's prints were clear, and they were followed, across the railway line, over a field, and across the frozen canal, over the coaching road, into the rocky woods where his trail was lost. He had come about four or five miles, over water, field and hills, and he must have carried his gains with him as he swam the river. To us he was a legendary fox, a brigand fox, a fox out of Grimm's fairytales, who wore a scarlet coat and showed his long white teeth, and perhaps he was a relation of Red Riding Hood's wolf.

To scare foxes away—and everybody with hens or ducks is alarmed at the depredations of the foxes—one should hang up black and green bottles to swing in the wind near the hen place. I am told this is a 'proper scarer'. To frighten pigeons from a garden or cornfield, a red bottle is hung up. These two 'recipes for fear' remind me of the black feathers of the crows dangling gruesomely from the fences in Sussex around the cornfields in the month of August, swaying in the gales, as a warning to all birds. I noticed these at Birling Gap, in the wire which now takes the place of hedges.

SNOW IN JANUARY

An icy wind, then a profound stillness, a steel grey sky, and the trees waited as if they knew what was coming. Down came the flakes of snow, like falling leaves twisting as they fell, and we rejoiced and hoped they would stay. They covered the ground, and soon the air was opaque with the falling whiteness. The attitude of the people to snow is revealing. The country-bred enjoy it, for a time, they remember their own childhood's joys, and they know that snow is a warm covering for the earth, that it helps the winter oats, and ploughland. Along the road go teams of children with toboggans, their voices clear and bell-like in the silence of snow. A little wind rises, the snow has stopped, and the sun shines, reflecting from every crystal, making blue shadows under the trees and walls. A white glittering fleece of snow covers the fields. From the hornbeams float tiny seedcases, which lie in multitudes on the snow, like the flight of arrows from some elfin band. The curious shape of the seed, with its three short wings, is emphasised by the sun. The other trees have shed their fruits in autumn, but the hornbeam waits for winter, and chooses the days of snow, although I often see the seeds whirling like small parachutes from the crooked trees in the woods.

The beeches still hold their prickly cases, and on a day with a clear blue frosty sky, they hang against the sky like little, brown, petalled flowers on the branches, delicate as the twigs from which they are suspended. Long ago the beech mast had fallen. They have delicious oily nuts, and country children eat them. I pick them up, shell them, and eat them, but nobody else seems to enjoy them. My gardener told me of a woman who had salted them for dessert in the war when nuts were scarce.

The Toad

January 22nd. Snow still lies on the ground. Under the cushion of snow-covered pinks, by a hole in the wall, hides a toad. How safe and cosy he is in the fretted roots! I lifted the hanging curtain of grey foliage and peeped at him. He gave a shiver and a shake. So I put a piece of paper over him to keep him warm and dropped the curtain. A robin waited close by, watching me, deeply interested in all that I did.

This toad is a friend of mine. He sat in the blue forget-me-nots during the summer, looking out from the skyblue flowers at sun and wind and rain. We did not disturb him, but in autumn when these flowers had to be thinned and carried away he walked out of the cover. He kept an eye on me until the gardening was finished. Then he solemnly strode back again to his green abode.

One very wet night of heavy rain I opened the back door to look for any flooding that might have occurred. In the darkness I saw the toad, squeezed against the doorpost. Perhaps he also wished to escape the flood on the stone pathway. He turned and walked away at once, but later when again I opened the door to look for him, there he sat, squeezed up in comfort. He strolled off, unwilling to enter. At midnight I peeped out, and there he was, so I left him. One night he came to the front door and sat there, sidling quickly away when the Scottie came out. As Gabriel Oak remarked, when he found a toad close to his home; 'He knew what this direct message from the Great Mother meant.' Now he has found new quarters in the shelter of the pinks where he will stay during the coldest months, undisturbed by me. For after the toad's visit, a great storm and flood followed. So my toad came up two steps to the dry doorstep to escape the flood on the pathway—the wise toad.

JANUARY FLOWERS

Deep snow has covered most of England and the roads here in Buckinghamshire have been nearly impassable, at least for me. My daily help cannot get through the drifts in her lane, and I am left alone. Now the snow has gone and an intense green-ness suffuses the earth, for we had almost forgotten how bright is the green in winter. Vivid streaks of emerald flow down the beech boles, as if a paint-brush had dipped down the trunks spilling the bright young colour carelessly, and the bare wood has a shimmer of green like spring when the sun shines on the wet boughs. I rush out to lift the branches of the magnolia, for the slender arms sweep to the ground, bent under the weight they have held in their thick leafy hands. This is a young giant magnolia I planted in the war and although it grew very slowly during the first years it has suddenly sprung outwards with great vigour. It has no flowers and I may have to wait for years to see the ivory cups. The glossy leaves with their nut-brown undersides make a winter decoration in a wooden bowl with lemons among them.

Now the fir trees are out of shape, a rosemary is smashed with the weight of snow, branches of the spirea are broken. This is the spirea arguta, which we call 'Bridal Wreath'. It is a prolific bush, about thirty years old, and it grows in a dull sunless corner, but it never fails in its miracle of snow-covered trails of delicate flowers which spring from the trunk like foam. I picked some twigs in December, black sprays with only a few leaves, but in three days they were smothered in white flowers.

The apple trees caught the snow and held it on every twig, so that the intricate tracery of boughs was black and white. The hawthorns and blackthorn bushes carry branches like white coral, stiff and angular, and I wish I could paint their Japanese shapes. The cherry trees overhanging the road by my gate were in full bloom of bunches of snow-cherryblossom, held up against a blue sky. Cherry trees are the most spectacular of snow trees in winter, but all trees are extraordinary in the winter snow.

This is the time of year when one searches for any sign of spring, knowing that winter has a long way to go, yet half believing it has turned away and forgotten to stay. Today, as I lifted the drooping broken plants I discovered a marvel. A brilliant blue gentian is flowering with the purest celestial flame, in the little rock garden. Its stiff trumpet lies parallel to the ground and the snow is held off by a broken cloche, for many cloches were smashed in the snow and wind. The mice and birds have eaten all the alpine crocuses, and half eaten bulbs lie forsaken.

Under a cloche are the snow-white flowers of the Christmas rose, Helliborus niger, late in flowering this year, but in a few days they will be tall enough to gather. The winter honeysuckle is out, with small balls hanging over the Hellibores, tiny flowers which disappoint me by their insignificance, although their scent is delicious in the house. The aconite, half hidden under its cut leaves, is a patch of deep gold with the round balls held in frills of green, like ruffs. On January 9th I saw the first flower.

Parkinson, in his *Paradisi in Sole*, calls the small aconite the Winter Wolfsbane. 'And first of the Winter Wolfsbane, which for beauty as well as the earlinesse of his flowers, being the first of all others that shew themselves after Christmas, deserveth a prime place.' He goes on: 'This little plant thrusteth up divers leaves out of the ground, in the deepe of Winter oftentimes, if there be any milder weather in January, but most come only after the deepe frosts, bearing up many times the snow upon the heads of the leaves.'

Aconites should be planted thickly in open woodland, or grass under trees, when they make a carpet of rich yellow. As children we used to see them filling the parkland under the trees at Haddon Hall, the Duke's Elizabethan house where we walked in spring. I think those flowers had been there since Elizabethan times, growing in that sheltered land, and we picked big bunches on our way to Dorothy Vernon's door. We thought of the Tudors, and the flowers with their green ruffs and stiffness of deportment seemed to belong to that other life which was not so far away from our own. At any moment the ghost of John Manners might appear and ask what we were doing, but we had a pass to that fairyland of Haddon.

Another memory of that house was the sweet blue violets that grew on the grassy turf of the banks, so deliciously scented that we went down on hands and knees with our noses to the earth. The colour was deep purple-blue, and I have some of the same variety springing up wild in my garden, blooming in January, creeping close to the soil among the stones until they are dragged out, for they move very swiftly as they try to invade the flower beds. On Christmas Day I picked some of these scented violets in the stone path of a Buckingham mill-house, blue flowers growing without any apparent soil to feed them, for they love the stones and crannies. In my search for winter flowers I went to the woodland at the end of my small garden, for signs of snowdrops. A few are showing their sharp pale green spikes, which pierce the hard ground, but no flowers are out. This is the winter flower, the epitome of January and February, and when I see the tight little bunches of closed buds in the shops and I smell that strangely moving scent of snowdrops, half bitter, half earthy, my heart misses a beat. They appear on the greengrocer's shelf, so small, so quiet, with a few ivy leaves round them, so modest among the freesias and the hyacinths, but they are quickly snapped up and the rich flowers are left. This is a week or two before they come out in my garden. Snowdrops do not increase and thrive here as in my old country home. They live happily, but they do not spread. They come up through the grass and birds tear their petals and perhaps grey squirrels eat the bulbs. The one place where they flourish is on the grave of my old Scottie, Hamish, by the stone which says: 'In memory of a faithful friend, Hamish, 1944.' It is a superstition that nobody must ever gather a flower which grows on a grave. So little Hamish enjoys the wealth of snowdrops and I am sure his rare spirit frisks and plays among them as he hunts for a shadowy bone.

Snowdrops have nostalgic memories for me, more than any other flower, except the tea rose. I was brought up with them, a company of white-skirted green-edged children, and they must have been the first flowers I saw. They were regarded always with a wonder at their bravery, as they pierced the deep, hard snow in the exposed orchard ground and held up their white heads when we broke the icy crust to find them in their hundreds. We squeaked with excitement to see them there, but we waited for the snow to melt before we gathered them.

The snowdrop may not be truly wild although in the Lake District they grow in great profusion and are apparently not descended from garden flowers. What is this wildness? How long does it take to be wild? In the rocky cliffs of Derbyshire I found them, and in the same rough ground I found the sweet blue violets so heavily scented one could detect their presence before seeing the flowers. Old writers do not mention snowdrops, Shakespeare misses them out, Gerard speaks of them as being wild in Italy, Parkinson ignores them.

The narrow green band on the flower, the suggestion of green in the whiteness of the petals adds to the beauty and enhances the fragility and poetry of the snowdrops. The closed bud is like a drop of snow, but when the petals open, the mystic three, and disclose the pencil of green on the whiteness, it is a secret revelation, something for each one to behold, alone. The French, *pierceneige*, is as descriptive as our own word, snowdrop, when the thin green spear which seems to be enclosed in a sheath of ice, pushes through the frozen earth with a surprising strength.

Every country cottage grew snowdrops when I was a child. The flowers hung their tiny heads in the smallest gardens, and some cottage gardens were only strips under a kitchen window, with rocks and ferns, with primroses and snowdrops and nothing else. Children carried the tight bunches to school and gave them to the teacher. We went every day to gather our snowdrops from the orchard. We sent them in the metal cups in the inner lids of the churns to the milkman in the great industrial town, and in boxes to friends. They went to tea-parties, they were put on graves, they appeared at winter birthdays, and they decked our table. Shopkeepers had bunches in their windows among the cakes, and this country habit remains in Buckinghamshire, where I often see the flowers in the baker's and confectioner's, singing their own quiet songs.

Yellow jasmine (Jasminum nudiflorum) has been in flower since November, and the long branches of yellow buds tinged with carmine open out in water in the warmth of the house to five-pointed stars. The snow and frosts seem to spoil the delicate flowers in the garden, the yellow petals are frozen, they become wan and transparent and the streamers of flowers appear to be destroyed, but a day of sun restores them and brings out new flowers. I cut the long twigs every day, for the jasmine is most accommodating. The flowers are lovely in black or bronze vases, they make a Japanese decoration as they spring out in natural curves which cascade like water.

The blue Blanda anemone is out, bending close to the ground as if to shield its little face from wind and rain. There are many of these to follow, pink and lavender, purple and azure, and they grow well on the rock garden, until they are crowded out. A white primrose and little Wanda primroses are here, and these

49

JANUARY

Wandas always seem to have a few starry flowers. The alpine crocuses are nipped off by birds and mice. Last year there were groups of Snowbunting and the gold and brown suzianus, but some of the bulbs have been eaten I fear.

January Garden Work

We have been pruning, the gardener climbing the ladder to snip the long thin whiskers of the apple trees, I on the ground, cutting back the roses on this day without snow or frost. I was converted to winter pruning three years ago, and each summer I get such a wealth of roses on strong stalks I am convinced this is the best time. So I choose a sunny day when there are no signs of frost—a rare day this—and work through the bushes. The old-fashioned roses must not be pruned, I am told, and Cottage Maid, Celestial, Helenae, send out long arching streamers to catch my hair and tangle my dress. Many of the species rose trees grow so fast I can foresee a tangle of roses, a wilderness of thorny branches, a forest of flowering fountains, with myself lost among them.

The moss roses grow with vigour, forming large shrubs which lean down like green people. William Lobb is there and the white moss, called Blanche Moreau, whose buds I gather and make into bunches, and the Rosa Mundi which is happy here, bearing flowers that cover the little trees, and Tuscany, deep dark crimson, and the York and Lancaster, which is disappointing, for I bought it simply for its tradition. All these must be untouched, although I am tempted to snip them shorter and as I prune the others, Hugh Dickson, thirty years old, from Cheshire, and La France, forty years old, and Peace and Lady Forteviot and many another, I imagine the roses in bloom. I spread leaf mould from the heap in the wood and some peat over the roots, and hope their feet are warm and their hearts strong.

The chief work in winter, in a haphazard half-wild garden like mine, is to pick up sticks in the wood for my fire, to sweep up leaves for leaf mould, and to make bonfires of the surplus, for nobody has the time and strength to gather up all the millions and billions of beech leaves that cover the ground several inches deep. We need not buy much kindling wood, for always there are fallen branches and broken boughs in windy weather lying up in the wood and they make fine crackling fires after they have been dried in the kitchen. After a storm I enter the wood and look round eagerly for the dropped firewood, which I gather up as if it were a present from heaven. It is surprising how many dead branches appear, as the trees grow and cast off parts they do not want.

The ground is golden brown with beech leaves, and we ruffle our feet deep in the drifts to hear the lovely shirring sound as we walk, as we have done always, since childhood. Macduff rushes into the leaves, which nearly cover him, and he darts down and squeals and leaps about as he sees some small animal which always escapes him. We drag the leaves with a long wire rake and carry the masses to a wire enclosure to make leaf mould. It takes many weeks to gather the leaves, but it is an exhilarating task, and I go out every fine day to rake or to make several small bonfires when raking is too much for me. The rich brown leaf mould is ready in two years, so we have a stack newly gathered, and one half decomposed and one ready for use. I use no fertiliser with it, but leave it to the weather.

WINTER WALK

I went past the farm, which seems to crouch in the narrow valley, in the Bottom, golden-red and yellow in the sunshine. The small old red house, covered with ivy, has a narrow garden paling across the front, dividing it from the great yard. Three little dormer windows peep from the steep red roof to the farm buildings, and another dormer looks out from a side gable, at the country road that passes by. Across the yard, smothered with straw and the manure heap, along the cobbled way, are the cowsheds and stables and the great barn with its double doors through which I once saw a tractor with a full load of corn disappear as easily as a lady slips into a dwelling place.

Runner ducks, cocks and hens were scratching in the straw, paddling in the wet places, racing round the barn-end to the rick-yard, where the stacks of straw stand. It was a homely scene, down there in the hollow. Across the road was the open barn filled with carts and harrow, with plough and machines. At the back of the farmhouse, across the narrow croft is a gigantic walnut tree, which I always admire, for in every season of the year it has a beauty and majesty of its own. I love to see a walnut tree by a farmhouse. It seems as natural and right for it to be there as for a rose tree to grow on a cottage wall.

I went along the narrow cart track, between two hedges which are being cut. They have overgrown to such an extent with lack of labour, that I am curious to see how they will be layered. The spindle tree from which I gathered masses of orange and cherry-coloured berries in the autumn, has been cut down.

I went under the railway line, through one of the curiously twisting tunnels which one sees about here, and up the hill through the wood by the rough lane. The ground is chalk, slippery in winter, and the trees are white beam, and dogwood, hazel and spindle wood. The hazel catkins were fully out in some places, and the dogwood was deep crimson. The hedges rise from banks about four feet high, for the lanes are sunk below the levels of the fields on either side. These banks are filled with flowers in spring, but in winter they are just as lovely with creeping ivy.

The ivy in the lanes flashes like diamonds, it glitters in the sunlight, and every little pointed leaf is alive and shining on a winter's day. The long trails drop from the earth, and fall in fountains down the banks, making the most perfect screens for the nests of birds. I have often been amazed at the curtain which conceals the narrow openings in the banks. Field mice run behind the leaves, birds build their nests, secure from human gaze, and the shielding ivy must keep off the wind and rain in those tiny homes.

JANUARY

There are orchards of apple and cherry up these lanes in the lower Chilterns, and public footpaths, bounded by fences, go among them, so that in autumn one can pick up a ripe apple from under one's feet, dropped from the boughs overhanging the path. On this winter's day I saw a fine piece of hedge-layering, which was different from that in other parts of the county. The hedge was very tall and overgrown, and the hedger had planted his stakes in the ordinary way, two feet apart, and drawn the long thin shoots of hazel and ash through them, without cutting them, bending the flexible saplings in curving lines, first to the right and the next group to the left, as he thought best. So the hedge was a decorative pattern of sweeping curves, ten saplings spreading like a fan to one side, and then a dozen or so drawn to the other side, and every one threaded through several upright stakes in weaving pattern. It was a thing of beauty, a real piece of craftsmanship, and I longed to be able to put the design on paper. This high fence bounded one of the apple orchards, by the side of the lane, in a lonely place where nobody would notice it, and it is so dense with its weaving no animal could get through it, and the little pigs and the sheep inside are safe as if a wall were round them.

At a demonstration of hedge layering at an agricultural show in the north of England, two countrymen were amazed at the closeness of the layering and the intricacies of the branches. One of the men said: 'It would turn a ship.' He used the old pronunciation for 'sheep', which was once common in England.

'Turn a ship?' said the other. 'Why it would turn an ouzel,' (a blackbird).

FEBRUARY

All the months of the year,
Curse a fair Februeer

trips off the ready tongue of those brought up on weather lore, and poor February bears a burden of rhymes of warning. The barometer has been at a low record, and I could hardly believe my eyes when I saw the drop of pressure. Snow, hail, wind—surely this must presage a fine summer later on, by a law of compensation, which is man-made and not weather-made.

CANDLEMAS

February has two special feast days which shine out to lighten the dark month, with candles and valentines; Candlemas on February 2nd and St. Valentine on the 14th. Candlemas has a weather tradition, for it has long been regarded as a turning point in the winter.

If Candlemas Day be fair and bright,
Winter will have another flight,
If Candlemas Day be cloud and rain,
Then winter will not come again.

is a rhyme still quoted and chanted in Buckinghamshire. It is as important as St. Swithin's Day in July.

We also used the following forecast:

If Candlemas Day be wet and foul,
The half of winter's gone at Youle.

Candlemas is the Feast of Purification, with the Presentation of Christ in the Temple. Then the candles were lighted and I always light a pair in memory of candlelight which is a close part of life still in remote places with no electricity.

A prayer for Candlemas begins: 'O Lord Jesus Christ, bless Thou this creature of a waxen taper at our humble supplication and by virtue of Thy Holy Ghost, pour Thou into it an heavenly benediction.'

The word 'creature' is used for anything created, animate or inanimate. 'These Thy creatures of bread and wine.'

It is a word used in childhood for all those creations, those objects, neither animal nor human, endowed with life by the imaginative, the dolls, the Teddy Bear, the gollywog, the rag doll, the stuffed monkey, and the Boy Scout doll. The Lares and Penates of home were all creatures, beloved.

On this Candlemas Day there was feeble sunshine and pools of rain lay in the ruts of the ground, as we went through the bare woods to look for 'holes in the trees'. For holes in trees have a fascination that never palls, whether they be the tiny moss-lined crannies with a dead leaf or shell of snail, or the larger hollows where a child might hide, or a fugitive perhaps sought safety in earlier days. At Burnham Beeches there are ancient trees with deep cavities, primitive houses for those who wish to shelter from the rain, fascinating shells of the old trees, which must be known to the animal world and belong to them. Sometimes we walk there, and a child peers from out of a tree, enchanted with the fairytale atmosphere, but February is not a good month for this game.

The little holes which are specially numerous in sycamore and ash trees were our post-offices, once upon a time. We posted leaf letters, pebbles with a message inscribed upon them by a stone, our initials, a date, a word of Latin, and we dropped these down the hole for some future traveller to discover.

There was a time of affluence when we hid a halfpenny in a tree, and then on later journeys we looked into these same hiding-places to see if anyone had discovered the treasure. Sometimes we found the little coin months afterwards, but often we never even spied the hole, it had completely gone, covered with creeping moss and ivy, reclaimed by nature. Nevertheless, we had been an intimate and lively part of the woods, explorers and adventurers, and they were our spiritual home.

So today my friend and I walked in the woods to find holes, for she was illustrating one of my small books in which a tree-cavity was important, and I wanted to make a sketch too. There were many crooked trees with hollows, and moss of every kind, silvery-olive moss, furry moss, golden-headed moss, little plates of pewter-coloured lichens, patches of silver-gilt, small toadstools and many a trophy. We came away with hollow branches which the wind had blown down, and silvery cushions of moss, round and compact, complete as miniature pouffes.

At night we lighted the candles, and set them on each side of a moss-lined dish with toadstool, and wet pebbles of quartz and pink granite, and small growing seedling trees, a miniature wood.

GARDENERS

Gardeners are elusive, especially the jobbing gardener, whose horticultural profession is only a side line. He has another profession, and gardening is only an incident to provide extra money, in a career dedicated to grounds-man, cricketer, post-office work, carpentry or farmwork. He comes when he likes and goes when he wishes. He has to go to town to buy his daughter a vanity case, or his grandson a toy horse. He has to put out the flags for the school sports, or prepare the ground for a Sunday cricket match, or fetch his Old Age Pension, or do his wife's shopping. So we wait and nobody comes, and we struggle alone.

One day he returns, hurrying to the garden shed, scurrying out with wheelbarrow and tools, scratching the earth and rattling the rake with vigour. There is inordinate joy about a visit from him, and I go to talk of flowers and plants and trees. He is concerned about a football pool and we discuss the chances of making a fortune. He gives his views about the iniquities of his neighbour at the Flower Show, and one realises that one can buy an exhibit.

We ask why he has not been for so long, and much injured he explains that he has not been well, he is still poorly, and the doctor told him not to go out to work but he knew you were in a fix so he came. The ground is too wet, too dry, it isn't the time for this, for that. Wait till the spring, the summer, the autumn. Then he smiles and his good-natured red face, his bright eyes, win the day.

My gardener has lumbago. We have been discussing remedies of which there are many up and down the country, and neither of us mentioned the doctor and the Health Service. He says juniper and gin, so I bought him a little bottle of juniper essence to be taken on sugar, and I thought of the juniper trees on the great hill by Wendover with their blue silk berries. Surely they could cure lumbago, for there is magic even in their beauty.

A nutmeg in the pocket is said to be a preventive, or a little bottle of quicksilver in the hip pocket, or even a raw potato. Some people wear a metal ring on the finger, iron not gold, and some have a chamois leather round the waist next to the skin or salt-petre in their shoes. Red flannel was worn half a century ago for lumbago, for red flannel had great powers of combating illness. The patient's back ironed with a hot iron is a well-known remedy, but perhaps a dangerous one for amateurs. This is such a painful illness, common to people who have to dig and stoop, gardeners and labourers, that uncommon methods have long been used to try to cure it. Goose grease, that ancient liniment known to every countryman, is also used for lumbago. We kept a pot of this ointment in a corner medicine cupboard ready for emergencies. What a strong odour came from this old painted cupboard, with its pills and salves and powders, and its remedies for everything!

SPELLING

Today I have had a letter from an old retired man who used to work for me, a wizened little countryman like a winter apple, with a nutcracker face, with no teeth, but with shining blue eyes like jewels, and a hobbling walk, a delightful little gnome out of Rackham's illustrations. He weeded my garden on his hands and knees, or squatting on his haunches, using a penknife. He seldom had any other tool, he was like the French peasants whom one sees in the courtyards of old houses in Provence, digging away with blunted knives in the crannies of cobblestones. He only stood upright when I called him, he was always bent double, working behind bushes, lost among the delphiniums and roses. I missed him very much when he retired at the age of seventy-five.

This is his charming note, thanking me for the birthday present I had sent to him.

'Madham, hoping you have got over the flue by the time you recive this letter thanking you most kindly for the fruet you sent us along.'

I always enjoy original spelling in a letter, and I do not consider it is illiterate. It resembles the seventeenth century way of writing, when each man showed his own individuality by his choice. Recently I came across some Elizabethan spelling.

'that famos felosefer Pathagarus and our gonores gave fiere,' (our gunners gave fire). And in the *Verney Letters* there are some delightful examples of originality.

I feel honoured to get this letter which must have meant a struggle with pen and ink, with rheumatic hands and poor eyesight, a table full of dinner things and no space to write. The old man and his invalid wife live in an ancient cottage at one of the 'Ends' of this town where four main roads cross. I thought they were very romantic highways when first I came here, and I am still fascinated by their names. London End leads to London, and Aylesbury End to the county town, Windsor End is the way to Windsor and the Castle, and Wycombe End is the road to High Wycombe, Oxford and the Cotswolds.

St Valentine's Day

Flakes of snow and flurries of wind, icy airs, and sharp hailstones heralded St. Valentine's Day, and even the robin was not there to sing on the gable end of the shed before he flew down for his breakfast. Three valentines came by post early in the morning, and I was wakened by the postman rapping and banging at the door.

'A very miserable cold day,' said he, as sleepily I took my parcel. All sleep fled when I opened it, and found a damp box lined with moss, and filled with flowers from a college garden at Cambridge. There were snowdrops, and the heart-shaped leaves of celandines, although none of the flowers yet, and pink small hyacinths and many-coloured St. Brigid anemones, for St. Bride's Day, which we forget. All wet and fragrant, they were lovely beyond compare this dark cold morning. I put them in an earthenware bowl, and went back to my warm bed to gaze at them. The robin sang, he was there after all. In the box, I later found a little painting of celandines and violets, with 'Febuary 14' neatly printed on it. The word February is a defeating word, the 'r' seems an intruder, and all my childhood years I said 'Febuary', with never a correction, for everybody else said the same. So I smiled at the card, and the way of spelling, which I would be the last to criticize.

The second card came from a countryman who can reap and plough and thresh and make a chair and sing a song. He had just had his eighty-fourth birthday, so, feeling young, he sent me a valentine with a couple of hearts and forget-me-nots and lace.

> *First to say you're very dear*
> *In hundreds of different ways,*

it began.

The last was from my son, another heart with the label: 'A valentine for one I love.' This has a teasing rhyme which pleases me inordinately.

> *I've always been so fond of you,*
> *To me—you're just divine,*
> *And now I've told you this, my dear,*
> *You'll be my Valentine.*

Our childhood valentine, always the same, as we printed and painted the rose and violet, had the words,

> *The rose is red, the violet's blue,*
> *Honey is sweet and so are you.*
> *Thou art my love, and I am thine,*
> *I chose thee as my Valentine.*

Later in the day three robins were dancing attendance upon one another on the lawn, and blackbirds were chasing each other, in a manner that was not friendly. Perhaps it was courting. On February 15th I heard the first song of the blackbird, in the evening after rain. The blackbird calls up the rain, say the gardeners. Soon the song will begin in the morning, but this evening song is very sweet and brave.

FEBRUARY ·

Pale gold wintry sunshine, with a blue sky and scudding clouds, and a strong wind blowing, came after days of rain, so I drove along a lane to see the bare woods in the new golden light, and to visit a certain hedge which pleases me winter and summer with its diversity. It divides the road from a wood, and it is neither hedgerow nor fence, but a low uneven wall of earth and great stumps of trees completely hidden in grass and flowers in summer; but from it grow ivy tods and young beech trees and small hollies, all dwarf and gaily-coloured like a row of stalls at a fair. A deep ditch separates this hedge from the road, and in February it is full of water. It is February Filldyke. Big lorries swing and sway along the narrow winding road of past enchantment, like dragons and prehistoric monsters. It is not their kind of lane, and they are invaders. In the wood we are cut off as if in another world, with the ditch between. Hazel catkins, green shoots of honeysuckle, golden brown beech buds, emerald moss studded with nodding seeds are the signs of spring.

The ivy berries on the broad bank of trees and grass this February day are purple as daphne, rich as plums; glossy leaves are differently shaped on each of the stout little bushes. Some are like squat hands, and some like the hands of musicians, some have a third finger that points out the beauty, some are ruddy, and some olive. Every little ivy tod is perfect like a bunch of green roses, and I gather a cluster, standing with one foot on each side of the ditch.

The brown beech leaves still cling to the branches of the tiny trees, and in this lane they remain soft tawny gold, warm as a little fire burning in the hedge. In summer the leaves are more delicate and of finer texture than ordinary beech, and in autumn there is always a cluster of gilded leaves striped with crimson, gayer than anywhere else. The hedge gets full sunlight, and the shelter of the wood behind.

The wood itself is an unknown land to me, I have never explored it, the verges and this hedge are all I want, with their diversity of colour and form. Sometimes we come here to sketch the twisted trunks of the miniature beeches and oaks, and to stare curiously at the many kinds of moss with cup and bead growing under the trees.

On this day of early February I went down the zigzag curve of the road, past the Magpies Inn, which has the sign of two pies, 'two for joy', painted afresh. This is a halting place for many travellers who come along the quiet road. It was mentioned by Thomas Ellwood, the Quaker, in the seventeenth century, for he lived not far away. Up the hill we drive, and along the crest by the water-tower. The view is very fine, a distant vision of azure and indigo fading away to the horizon. Amersham lies in the valley below, and as we enter it on this cold day it emits a radiance, a warmth and homeliness and an air of comfort: England personified.

The little town stretches along a broad High Street; the space between the two sides of the road is broken by the Guild Hall built on open arches with pillars holding up the room above. The diversity of roofs and windows, doorways and chimney stacks, is so great that every kind of dwelling place seems to be here, from almshouses in the tiny courtyard, to Queen Anne houses and Manor House and the tiniest house of a fairytale with one up and one down—'Wee Oak'. The roofs particularly, of red tiles, mossed and lichened, crinkled and waved, are a manifestation of the individuality of human beings. For every house is unique, some as small as the woodcutter's cot in Hans Andersen, some large and stately with fine doorways and many windows. One little house has wall-paintings of the sixteenth century in the front room, and there are panels of Julius Caesar and the rest of the Nine Worthies. Another has Elizabethan twisted chimneys. We walked down the High Street, looking at these shops and houses, the inns, the arched doorways into courtyards, through which there are glimpses of fields and woods. A house with an overhanging storey was once a blacksmith's forge but now it is a shop, and the cobblestones from the floor have been removed to make the yard. The Griffin Inn has little rooms, and a courtyard. The Crown Hotel is Elizabethan, with a later frontage, and in the dining-room there was until recently the painted coat of arms of Queen Elizabeth, 'God save the Quene', with the Lion and Dragon. It was burned in a fire and only a copy remains. The courtyard has a large grapevine and a mighty honeysuckle which embowers the ancient walls and buildings.

We called at a little corner shop, heaped with apples from the three orchards of the owner. There was no artifice in the arrangement. Apples lay in piles of rosy and yellow fruit, at a few pence a pound. An enamel bowl held bright green watercress, freshly picked from the cress-beds in the river. This neighbourhood is famous for its watercress, and for wooden utensils, made of beech and ash, turned in the small mills at Chesham. So I carried off a smooth wooden spoon of beechwood for my cooking. There is a satisfaction in using a wooden spoon, or a well-turned bowl of wood, or a wooden fork, especially when it has been fashioned at a lathe by an open door and a stream runs near to give the power. I once visited the little factories where these spoons and bowls were made and I met some of the craftsmen, so I have a great interest in them.

Last of all we went to a shop with the sign of a great iron cooking pot over the door. It is kept by a countryman I know well. We can wander about and talk of country life with someone who shares one's interests, and remembers tales of his father's time. As we talk we look at his stock of Staffordshire pottery, with Robin Hood and Maid Marion, with King Lear and Hamlet, Mr. Shakespeare standing with a book and Mr. Wesley preaching in a pulpit. There is an assembly of shepherds and huntsmen, Babes in the Wood and Red Riding Hood and the wolf. Our friend knows the history of each, and he tells us of the cottage mantelpiece where the treasured bits of 'chiney' have lived all his lifetime, to be sold in the end as there is nobody to inherit them and money is scarce. Once I bought a pair of china dogs with gold chains round their necks which had belonged to an old lady, his aunt, who loved them. She wanted them to go to an owner who would take care of them, not to a dealer from London. Now they stand on my kitchen mantelpiece, a distinguished pair, one with gold spots, the other with dark green lustre spots, and each with an air of disdain.

Today I chose a Rockingham china cottage white as snow, inexpensive because the chimney has been mended. I do not mind a lack of perfection, for I am no collector. It has open windows and little round dove-cot holes where infinitesimal pigeons can fly in and out, like the house dove-cots in some Buckinghamshire villages. It has a tiny dog kennel by the door and a small white rain-barrel to catch the imaginary torrents and to supply the house with water. It would look correct if placed on the green moss in the beech wood and left for some bemused child to discover, for it is that kind of exquisite little cottage. Then, with Rockingham cottage and ivy tods glittering with berries, with watercress and apples and a wooden spoon, I drove home along the lovely valley and over the steep hill, well content with my shopping in beech wood and little old town.

FEBRUARY FLOWERS

Early in the month the twigs of the Forsythia were clustered with prickly beaks of fledgling flowers, yellow as the bills of young thrushes. I gathered some sprays to add to the lime-yellow of hazel catkins, which now adorn the trees in many a lane, for the starry flowers and the delicate catkins come out together. The tiny scarlet tassels of the hazel are on the twigs, and the catkins which are stiff and undisclosed are tinged with red. The ivy with very small leaves, perfect in shape, but like doll's ivy, grows on the little crooked trees in a poor little wood, which will soon be cut down for building I fear. This ivy is encrusted with the brightest green moss, and the flat webbed hands clutch the trees, holding so tightly I can scarcely draw them away. The green fingers move up the trunk, carrying scraps of earth, caught in their grasp, and they glow with light on a winter's day when all else is dark. Rose-red leaves, tawny-gold, emerald, jade, the colours are theirs, on the whiskered stems which clamber from the mossy bank to the trees. Ivy is suburban, but the Elizabethans liked it, and decorated their houses with it, mingled with holly. On the ground it makes a strong network which holds the crumbling soil together, and its enamelled surface shines out in the darkness of woods.

In the garden aconites are out, and snowdrops, and delicate blue and white alpine crocuses, miniature cups of light. Yellow crocuses shine from under the wood, where the birds leave them alone. In the garden they are soon torn to shreds. On the small rock garden the Pulchella Violet Queen tulips carry their royal bishop's purple, and azure and lavender and rose anemones, the Blanda anemones, are out.

A few little Iris Reticulata have pierced the earth and spread out their petals, and the Daphne Mezereum is in bloom. The angular and contorted branches of Japonica have only a few round buds instead of early flowers, as the tree was cut too late in autumn.

For the first time I have grown Dog's Tooth violets, the Erythronium Denscanis, an exquisite and graceful flower with leaves of great beauty covered with a network of lines, and mottled like a frog. The flowers resemble miniature lilies, and the white dog's tooth violet is a small marvel, with hanging heads pretending to be lily-buds. They are flowers with an element of surprise as they curve up on their coloured stalks and open their long petals.

'This is not a violet,' exclaim visitors indignantly, and I excuse the name and try to discover the resemblance between the shapes of the buds and the teeth of my Scottie.

The solitary flowers hang down their heads with six long narrow petals, which 'turning themselves up again, after it hath felt the comfort of the Sunne,' says John Parkinson, 'that they doe almost touch the stalks again.' The 'comfort of the Sunne' is what we all desire.

'The flower hath no sent at all, but commendable only for the beauty and forme thereof,' he says. The beauty and shape are of the highest order of grace and wonder.

FEBRUARY

ROBINS

In the snow days of this February I had a letter from a village near my childhood home in Derbyshire, telling me of the beauty of the hills, where each evening when the sun sets the snow is pink under the diffused light of the west. This rosy light shines on a high ridge of wood and field stretching to the horizon, a hill I once thought to be the world's end, the last barrier between earth and heaven.

I have seen coal-tits in the garden, the greater spotted woodpecker, thrushes, blackbirds and chaffinches. Two robins are here every day, and one of them often flies through the window to settle on the back of a chair or on a picture frame. It is interested in human life, it makes no effort to escape, or to find food, but there it stays watching me as I move about.

A few days ago I listened to Ludwig Koch on the radio, as I sewed. He said he was going to play a record of a robin singing, so I quickly opened the french window and left it slightly ajar. It was very cold, but I thought a robin might be near. The bird song began, I looked across the room, and a robin entered. It stood in the doorway, its head cocked towards the radio about twenty feet away. Then it joined in the song, and when the record finished it went out, with never a glance at me. The human voice of Ludwig Koch on the radio disconcerted it. The recorded song of a thrush followed, and back came the robin, staring at the corner of the room from which the notes rang out, but not venturing to explore. Again, as the human voice commented on the bird-song in the record, the robin hopped back to the garden. A third time it came to hear the record of the dunnock's song. It listened intently, and both the robin and I stared at the radio, for I felt too that I shared the little creature's wonder and surprise. Ludwig Koch spoke, and away to the garden went the robin, and there it sang its own sweet musical song. It sang most deliciously and loudly, rippling through its notes, and I sat quietly here, enjoying the little concert it gave to show me what it could do.

FEBRUARY

Coleridge, speaking of the robin, says: 'He, sweet cock-my-head-and-eye, part-bashful darling, that makes our kitchen his chosen cage.'

Another robin makes my kitchen his cage. He comes from the east side of the house, in at the open door, but he is a seeker after crumbs, not a distinguished companion like the north-side robin. He flies in, he does not hop through the door, and he only sings in the tree outside, or on the fence, but he greets me every morning with the same insistence as the bird at the french window on the north side.

There is a fashion to deride the robin, perhaps because it appeared on Victorian Christmas cards with ivy and holly, or because it has been too popular with simple people. We are told that no bird is more unsuitable for a card at Christmas, for the robin, they say, is lacking in goodwill. He is called an 'aggressive brute', a 'flattering bird', who has a dark side to his character. He is said to be greedy and to tolerate human beings solely for food. With this I cannot agree, for again this is giving human attributes to the bird. Goodwill to man, religious feeling, brutes and flatterers are not part of the bird kingdom. I am sure the robin is not greedy, for his friendliness has another source—curiosity, not food. I have lain out in the garden recovering from illness, and a robin has stayed near me, to entertain me, for there was no food about. He came close, perching on my rug, sometimes singing a stave, and gazing about with his inquisitive eye. Each day he flew down from the tall oak tree to a post in the raspberries, and then, looking at me as if to ask if he might come nearer, he dropped to the ground and stayed with me.

He perches on the handle of the fork, he flutters round the gardener turning up the soil, through curiosity alone. He is like my Scottie who is not interested in food but in human beings, for he likes me to dig holes with him, to wheel barrows for him to chase, and to go through doors for him to follow. The robin never takes the garden fruit, he is the most polite of birds.

FEBRUARY

George Darley, the poet, and the friend of Charles Lamb, wrote a quiet dirge for the death of a robin, a grief we have often experienced.

> *A little cross*
> *To tell my loss.*
> *A little bed*
> *To rest my head;*
> *A little tear is all I crave*
> *Upon my very little grave. . . .*
> *I strew thy bed*
> *Who loved thy lays;*
> *The tear I shed,*
> *The cross I raise,*
> *With nothing more upon it than*
> *'Here lies the little friend of man.'*

The robin has his own territory, indeed many birds have their own territories which they defend, as dogs have their boundaries in the garden and human beings have their own houses and living space. The robin is the little watch-dog of the garden, but he tolerates other birds. When a crowd comes to the bird table, the robin stands apart, and waits till they have finished before he ventures near to take a crumb. If he is at an unoccupied bird table he flies away when another bird comes to eat and remains on a tree until the second bird has gone. I have watched him for many hours and never have I seen him chase away a bird. Blackbirds, tits and sparrows, starlings and chaffinches chase neighbours, but not the robin.

He is recognised as the Christmas bird, not because he has been so often painted by sentimentalists, with his red breast against the snow, but because he is so conspicuous in our fields and gardens, on hedges and lawns, where he comes, not for food, but for companionship. He has that odd affection for human beings that dogs and cats and horses possess, an interest in their queer ways, a curiosity about their goings-on. He gazes into the house from the windowsill, he feels the texture of silk

68

and wool, of warm wood and polished piano top, he slides his feet on the ivory keys, and touches the brass curtain rail taking a thousand impressions of our life, so strange and rare and unpredictable to a bird. His zest in following the gardener, even perching on the handle of the spade, which is a favourite resting place, warm for his toes, smelling of the person who held the tool, is not necessarily greed for a worm, although he does not disdain the titbit which is turned up. He joins in the game of gardening as my Scottie does, each one in his own way sampling the work and play of man—the robin singing lustily and hopping around, the dog racing after the wheelbarrow's revolving wheels, chasing the lawn-mower. How strange is the animal man to use these tools, tearing up the ground which holds worms and lost bones and stones and other treasures!

On February 11th I saw a robin singing on the head of the leaden boy riding on his dolphin, and the statue seemed to share the joy of it. For a statue gives the impression a garden is inhabited. Every day now the robins enter the house.

On this date too I heard the green woodpecker 'laughing', the first time this year, and snow fell instead of rain. Every night owls screech, like wild children calling to one another. It is a sound that intoxicates me with a queer kind of bliss, like certain music—Stravinsky, De Falla—for there is something outside time, beyond reality in the owl's cry.

On February 7th there was a great chatter of little birds, a squeak and a flurry of bright wings in the wood, as a flock of finches darted here and there, so I went across the lawn to see what was the matter. I expected to find a cat, but on a bare beech tree were three tawny owls. One was close to the tree trunk, and the light of the sun on tree and bird camouflaged it miraculously, so that the flecks of brown on the bough and on the bird's back were the same shade. Another owl sat up in the tree and looked at me very sternly, and its beak was almost cream in the sunlight. The third owl was restless; it flew a short distance with the silent flight that is so beautiful, sudden and easy as a feather floating through the air. The cry of the little birds continued, in spite of my presence. Then the sky darkened, pewter-coloured clouds swept across and hail began to fall.

As I lie in bed I can hear the owls calling across the lawn, and nothing is more entrancing than that strange, wild cry, which I have heard all my life, and exulted in. It is haunting, eerie, uncivilised, but sometimes it is warm and friendly. Then I think I am safe with shutters closed, and horses and cattle in their building and all the world contained in a nutshell.

The thrush has returned to the beech tree in a garden near, a pollarded beech, and this is a special thrush for I heard it last year. It has a superb song, richer than that of other thrushes, with motifs of its own composition, a Bach, a Schubert of a thrush. The chaffinch sings but has not reached the 'no cheese' of the song.

My white-headed blackbird has not begun its song yet, but it bathes every day near the window; it squats on the snow.

THREE TREES

> *Tree-life is like a corridor between*
> *The Seen and Unseen.*
> *Trees are like sentinels that keep*
> *The passage of a fate*
> *From this sleep to that other sleep;*
> *Between two worlds they wait.*
>
> H. Monro.

In a hedgerow of hazel and dogwood, ash saplings and hawthorn a great beech tree stood out against the clear blue sky of a February day. There had been storms and much rain, and then a frost which silvered everything and froze the muddy pools but the morning sun melted the cat ice, and the lane was deep in soft dark mud. Above it rose this tree, a vivid almost speaking tree, it was so alive on this February day. There was a gentle movement, not from the wind, but from the tree itself, as if it were reaching up, stretching out its long sensitive fingers. The colour of the tree was silver, a cold, metallic shade, but the beautiful tree was triumphant there. I remembered it from occasional walks, for it is the only beech tree in the hedges round those fields. It stands close to a gate, and behind it the field rises to a crest, with a flattish piece out of sight. Once I climbed to see beyond, and the upper part of the field was ploughland, the lower slopes grass. In the grass in summer grew patches of blue chicory, as delicate as the sky in February.

The cold sunshine which turned the tree to silver, brought out faint golds and greens in another great tree, standing close to the farm in the valley. It is a walnut, of vast size, with spreading branches and many boughs.* I tried to count these, and fifteen thick boughs stretched out from the main trunk, spread like an umbrella of great coverage. This is a tree I visit quite often, for its colour changes in every light. I admire it the most when snow covers the ground and a frosty sun shines through the interlacing branches. The shadow of the tree lies on the snow, violet-coloured, or blue, with such a network of tracery it is a miracle of loveliness. I think the shadow is even more beautiful than the tree itself, but together they make something that should be kept in memory. How can I keep it, I wonder? How can I preserve this miraculous beauty, for no artist could paint it, no photograph could get the elusive colour, the inner life of the living tree, the light and shade of the thousand crossing twigs, each allowing a certain amount of sun to fall on the snow. The wood is silvery-white in some lights, and then it is rich green and gold. It is the most changeable tree, this rich old walnut, the last of a company of ancient walnut trees, some of which have been cut down, others have decayed and fallen. In high summer it has its special beauty of foliage and movement as it catches each breath of wind. In autumn the leaves look sad, as they fall heavily, but the tree throws them off with relief.

It is a family tree, belonging to the farm close to it. There used to be a swing on one of the boughs, but the children have grown to be young farmers, and no one plays there. A hen coop

* *The walnut tree has now been cut down.*

stands under it, cattle rub against it, a washing line stretches from it across the green to the farm. Faggots and pea-sticks and planks lean against it. A wheelbarrow is reared there, and a broken plough, and a chain harrow; it looks after its assembly of common homely things, as if it knew what it was doing. On this February day its roots were in the muddy earth, trampled by the cattle, and the intricate lacy shadow lay on the broken green and brown soil, but the tree's trunk was mottled with shadowed gold, and the twigs against the sky were silver as the twigs of the beech half a mile away.

I visited my third tree on this rolling hillside in Buckinghamshire, a tall larch. It was dark and forbidding, and dishevelled, with untidy twigs and little cones, and never a glimpse of the soft greens hidden there, of the red tassels and the delicate beauty. Larches in winter are depressing trees, they look as if nothing would induce them to have a leaf. They are sooty and grimy, and desolate as an untidy garden. Then, suddenly they spring to vivid life, and I wonder if any colour in the paint box can ever give that wet luxurious green of their own little brushes, or if any scent bottle can give that heady perfume which intoxicates me, and brings nostalgic memories of larch woods in childhood when one's senses were keen as those of the fox.

HEDGING

The hook is cutting the tall hedge, the saplings of ash and hazel, cutting wood for thatching spars too, ash, dogwood and hazel undergrowth. I walked across the paths to a lane where I can find catkins and many buds in the winter from the tall overhanging hedges, but this day I had a surprise, for the hedges had just been slashed, and a palisade of sharp white spear heads was there, a regular ambush along both sides of the lane. The brushwood lay in heaps in the fields ready to be burned. The long thin switches of hazel and willow were already twisted through the hedge, to make the impenetrable fence which is so pleasant to see. In one place the hedge had been cut clean away for some reason, perhaps because there were no saplings for binding. Here sharp stakes were driven into the top of the bank, each about four or five feet high, and the next day the saplings would be woven through them to make the basket-work pattern of the new fence. The banks of the muddy lane had been cleared and cleaned and I could see the green rosettes of foxgloves, the bright heart-shaped leaves of celandines, and the pointed spotted leaves uncurling in the winter sun of the Lords and Ladies, piercing the brown earth like spears. I followed the winding lane to see the hedging, some of it barely started, some of it quite finished. A well-known hedger and ditcher lives in the village near, and this was his work. Lower down the hill the hedge was so high and overgrown it seemed almost impossible that such a neat trim piece of work as this would be the result, but the days following and all the month of February he will work at the hedges round here. I think of my bushes of spindle, where I gather branches of the pink and orange berries in autumn, and I hope some of them will be left. It must be several years since this hedge was layered, but it had grown to such a tangle of trees and flowers and saplings one could scarcely penetrate it, and the lane was shadowed and covered with green. When the banks are free from their young trees—I have found many little cherry trees growing and flowering here—the flowers will have a chance, for this is a lane where the lovely dark blue bell-flower flourishes, and the deep claret corncockle, and balsams and teazle, with heavenly blue chicory, and purple orchis. Last year the flowers were lost in the heavy tangle of bushes, but now they will be free.

Stakes are inserted about two feet apart. Through them are woven the pliable branches of hazel and ash, only half cut so that they will continue their growth, and the topmost edge of the sharp uprights has a plaited basket-work along it, which is called 'eddering' or 'hethering' in Buckinghamshire.

In my childhood in Derbyshire there were more stone walls than hedges, and February and March were walling months. The men went to the fields to build afresh the breaks in the strong walls. There was an art in this, the stones had to be chosen very carefully, balanced, fitted, to make a sturdy wall to resist stormy winds which blew with such fierceness in the wild county of hills, to keep in jumping horses and sheep, and to restrain the careless wanderers who would climb a wall and try to dislodge the stones.

Hedges were not layered. They were slashed and trimmed, and the great trees which were part of the hedges were left to grow, for shelter. It was necessary to have high hedges there for refuge in winter storms, both for man and beast.

MARCH

Dear March, come in!
How glad I am!
I looked for you before.
Put down your hat.
You must have walked!
How out of breath you are!

—Emily Dickinson

Winter again! I awoke to snow, on the first day of March, a surprising sight, for the windows were iced in patterns of ferns and jagged diamond trees, and the air was sweet and exhilarating. March has come in like a snow-white lamb, with a fleece of snow and frost on its small pricked ears. Or is it really a lion in disguise?

The trees stood in ghostly silence, with never a breath, as if they had been transfixed with astonishment to see the powdered snow and the caps of ice. The light glitters on bush and stone and roof, the sun shone down on this brilliance, jewelling the ice

75

crystals, for the facets of the snowflakes flashed with red and green and blue, as I moved my head to catch the rainbows.

The great beech tree across the lawn was like a mighty fountain, caught by magic and frozen to immobility. The wood pigeon cooed as if in wonder at this change after the sun and showers of late February, when we thought winter had gone.

The sparkle was extraordinary, and perhaps one's eyes are more open to receive the split light on certain days. Sometimes perhaps we can act as a prism, and break up the white light into the many colours of the rainbow, I thought, as I stared at the snow, and caught the jewels of green and red. I remembered the woods through which I ran to school in childhood, on some such frosty morning, when the sun was low and the sun's rays struck almost horizontally. It was a fairyland of beauty, I was always enchanted, and sometimes awed by the great silence of the white woods which stretched so far in the distance as I stepped on untouched snow which hid my lonely pathway.

PLUMBERS

My thoughts suddenly veered most unromantically to the water-pipes, for I had already had two visits from the merry plumber and his mate, who unfroze my water-system. I hurried to turn on the taps, and all was well, the water flowed freely. 'Have you had the *plummer* yet?' was a question in one of my letters today.

In my childhood we were spared this anxiety which assails me throughout the winter, for there was no plumbing in the accepted sense of the word. The lead pipes in the kitchen were warm and safe, and friendly, for they were made from local lead, such as we saw in the veined rocks. They would never betray us. It was a primitive everyday experience in frosty weather to take an axe-head and break the ice on the surface of the water trough before we could boil the big copper kettle for breakfast, to splinter the ice and to throw a jagged piece on the stones for luck. Then a lading-can was dipped into the dark secret depths, and the water under the ice had a special quality, a mystery of cold, which excited me.

I should have enjoyed a visit from the plumber in those early days. If he had forgotten his tools, in the traditional way, he would have taken half a day to fetch them from the village, but I never met a plumber, he was a mythical person, with an odd name. Perhaps plumbers all live in the south of England, where the walls are thin and the windows many, and coal is dear, where the system of pipes run along the outside walls, showing their unabashed nakedness. Little cisterns are perched uneasily under the unlined roofs, and they freeze and freeze, as the wind blows down upon them. Plumbers are always on the doorstep, with bags of tools and blow-lamps, and pieces of piping. The young red-headed plumber's mate who once came is now the head plumber with a mate of his own. They climb through the trap door into the roof-space, and unfreeze the pipes which are wrapped in carpets and felting and old trousers, but the pipes freeze again with the next deep frost.

On this snowy March morning I went out to pick some sprigs of winter honeysuckle to scent the rooms, but the jasmine had its yellow petals curled and spoiled, with long streamers of flowers whitened by the frost. The little rock fuchsia which I rashly planted was stricken and dark so I hastily put a sack over it. I covered up all my precious plants again, the Romneya Coulteri, the passion flower, the camellias.

Out on the snow-covered lawn the blackbirds were crouching on the snow, their wings stretched as if they wished to get a close contact. Robins were at the bird table, with chaffinches and all the company, and a jay screamed in the wood, waiting for me to go away. The leaden boy at the edge of the wood looked very beautiful in the light, with a powdered cap on his head and snow in the fold of his arm. There was much life in the garden, with the Scottie and birds and the leaden boy to look on.

Sunshine on snow is a marvel, and the colour of spring came to the bare trees, the rosy dogwood, the green willows and the silver birches, each distinctly painted, as the rays caught the trunks and wavered upon them like water. Macduff was so excited by the feeling of spring and the glitter of snow, that he leapt clean over a little Peke who is an acquaintance, jumping high like a small black lamb, dancing and patting his paws, to the discomfiture of the sedate, aloof little aristocrat.

BONFIRES

March 4th. At night I went out to make bonfires of dead leaves in the little wood, with snow on the ground and frost in the air. The moon was shining through the bare trees, and the two fires, crackling and sending showers of sparks from the broken sticks which litter the ground, burned amazingly well. As darkness came, it was entrancing to look from the house at the two spires of grey smoke and the dancing flames in the distance, with the boles of the trees outlined against the fires, and in the foreground the crystal snow, sparkling in the moonlight, with footprints of human beings and dog and birds. Everything was very still, and cold and remote as Siberia, or so it felt in the silence of the sky. One can pretend the old games of Red Indians, or Russians in the Steppes, or primitive man when a fire burns in the snow and the moon looks down.

I found yellow crocuses out under the snow as I raked away the leaves, and snowdrops in the wood, and some long budded daffodils which were poking their green beaks out of the snow, and tufts of young camomile, all waiting for the sunshine.

DORCHESTER

We are a quarter of the way up 'March Hill', but the snow still covers some of the ground, and the winds are icy and bitter, while at night the frosts are keen. On this day, March 9th, snow fell with sleet added to it, and the roads were icebound early, although some of them thawed later.

We set off on a journey to Dorchester-on-Thames. We went

through High Wycombe with its traffic congestion, where we often meet a circus procession or a great lorry laden with trees. We passed through the lovely narrow village of West Wycombe, a National Trust village, where one can never linger to admire the houses and inns, for lorries and cars stream in an endless chain. On the snowy hillside above the yew trees, sombre and snow-decked stands the church of West Wycombe, with perhaps invisible strife of demons going on in the air above the great copper ball. We went up the long hill, beautiful in brown and pearly grey and white, with a farm and cattle in the valley, through Stokenchurch. The snow was so thick we had to stop on the summit to wipe the windscreen, but as we dropped down Aston Rowant hill into Oxfordshire the weather improved.

We went on, through the icy air which cut and stabbed with its thin fingers, to Dorchester-on-Thames, to see the great Abbey church, cold as the grave on this March day of bitter weather. In the East windows is stone carving, and a wonderful structure of a stone tree rising from the recumbent body of Jesse. The Jesse window is amazing with its foliage and saints and stories carved in stone around the glass. Mediaeval glass fills some of the panes of the great East window, others are modern. The lively, vivid, startling figure of the Dancing Warrior, a knight lying on a tomb, with eyes wide open, mouth grimly smiling, and legs twisted as if he were about to rise up and fight, or dance, or rush into our civilisation with his sword and bitter mouth, proclaiming his victory over death, is one I can never forget. I placed my hand upon him and kept it there, waiting to feel the throb of his heart, the beat of blood, the surge of life, deep in that ancient stone, for the touch makes a link between past and present; statues are like animals, they are aware of a human touch, and a word to comfort them and give them remembrance in the forgotten eternity where they dwell. So there I stood, secretly, with my hand on that writhing body of the unknown knight, under whose mailed feet even the little lion lay askew, struggling to escape from the pressure, its frightened tail between its legs. An unknown knight indeed, for even 400 years ago the name of this intense and vital man was forgotten.

On the floor near him were tombstones with good lettering, and the figure six in a curled spiral, like a shell, a convoluted six of the seventeenth century, a six I would like to adopt, for my own use and pleasure.

On one of the flat tombs I read a tribute to a young woman, and who could pass the spot without feeling a touch of a ghostly, beckoning hand? Standing there, in the ice-cold Abbey church I copied the words, shivering as I did so.

> 'Reader!
> If thou hast a heart fam'd for
> Tenderness and Pity, Contemplate
> this spot,
> In which are deposited the Remains
> of a Young Lady whose artless
> Beauty, innocence of Mind and gentle Manners
> once obtained her the Love and
> Esteem of all who knew her. But when
> Nerves were too delicately spun to
> bear the rude Shakes and Jostlings
> which we meet within this transitory
> World, Nature gave way. She sunk
> and died a Martyr to Excessive
> Sensibility.
>
> Mrs. Sarah Fletcher,
> wife of Captain Fletcher,
> departed this life at the village of
> Clifton on the 7 Jan. 1799.
> In the 29 year of her age.
> May her Soul meet that Peace in Heaven which
> this Earth denied her.

As I wrote this epitaph two young women came up, and one, a local girl, began to whisper to the other the details of the tomb.

I joined them, and she told us that a ghost had haunted the spot for many years, but now it was at peace. The young wife went mad and committed suicide in 1799. She was buried in unconsecrated ground outside the church. Her spirit haunted both church and graveyard and many saw her and were troubled by her. At last her body was removed from the unconsecrated ground, and she was given a burial inside the church at the spot where we stood. Her spirit then ceased its troubled wanderings.

We passed through the doorway in the great screen or partition that once divided the monks' part of the church from the small area reserved for the village congregation. On the wall above the altar is a fourteenth century mural, a painting of the Crucifixion with lovely curved bodies, swaying in grief.

The distant Berkshire Downs were blue as a delphinium in the afternoon light as we drove away, and the landscape was suffused with colour, lavender, indigo, straw-yellow, carnation, and the ivory of snow on the hills. It was a scene to marvel at, and to wonder whether this was our dun-coloured England transformed as if by a rainbow. Is the sight more keen on certain days, is the sense of colour more acute? Sometimes I stare in amazement at the colour of the country, but even when the tones and lights are radiant, they are dim compared with the beauty of landscape in dream, when an inner light comes from the substance of earth, a light shines through rock and grass and petal from nature herself illuminating every vein and crystal and frond.

We drove down the long hill towards Henley, and along the Fair Mile with its trees and surrounding woods, to Henley Bridge, where we stayed a few minutes to gaze at this structure of consummate beauty. Dorchester has a bridge of the same period and graceful shape, but Henley has its carved cutwaters and its fine lacy parapet.

We passed by lovely Hambleden, with its white ancient mill standing by the river, and its great weirs and many waterfalls, past Medmenham, the village of quiet enchantment, and through Marlow where the Thames is trained to obedience and taken through a weir and a lock in cascades of green water before it goes on its journey to London and the sea. We speeded along with no time to stop, but at one point on the road we saw a strange sight. A distant copse of dogwood was caught in the sun's long low rays so that every slender branch of the thousands of saplings was illuminated to rose-red. The effect was that of a great bank of red peonies growing tall, with a background of brown naked birch trees. Never have I seen such richness in dogwood as in that moment of crimson, when the slant of sun-rays and the reflecting surface of the saplings was perfect. Many passing motorists must have mistaken it for a display of rosy flowers, glowing in the snowy field.

THE STATUE

On a grey March day with bitter east wind and heavy sky, the little lead boy riding on his dolphin shines out, warm and richly-coloured, shaded with silver, on the deep purplish grey of the lead. How different he is from the sky we call leaden, and from the beech trees, whose trunks are also leaden, and how dark he is against the brown earth which has something of spring in its colour! His face is silvery, his left arm across his breast is light as air, he might easily wave it to the sky, and it always catches the gleam of sun, or the moonbeam or even starlight. It has a grace beyond beauty, an airiness, while the dolphin upon which the naked child rides is darkly shadowed, the thick scales and the grotesque head and the tail are in the deep waters of the sea of shade. A garden with a statue is inhabited, it is never lonely; there are beings enjoying the flowers day and night.

The rosemary bush near the statue has some of the leaden tones in its crooked boughs, and, oddly, it bends over with the same curve as the body of the child. In winter's snow this bush is weighted down with the burden on the thickly furred branches, so that it looks like a large dog crouched in the garden. Often I am startled to see it bending there with fierce aspect, but when the snow melts it raises itself and stands on its twisted trunk in a seemly manner. Now evening has come, and the leaden boy is like a shadow, he merges into the twilight, he is invisible. What unknown artist first made this lovely creature of the eighteenth century? Who fashioned the small foot curled back, hollowed under the instep? Who made the small body arched to show the little hollows in the back and the smooth roundness of the childish limbs? He is alive and listening with pointed faun's ears and eyes downcast to seek the spring of water down in the earth's depths.

Dairy Carvings

I drove to Marlow to a favourite shop where wooden utensils are sold, the every-day objects which once lay on the shelves of farm dairy and pantry and dark passages, as well as in the stone alcoves of barns and such places in my childhood days. Sieves and scoops of wood, yew, sycamore, box and beech, ladles for brewing, skimmers and gingerbread men moulds were there. An Elizabethan toothcomb made of boxwood had smooth even teeth for combing the Elizabethan child's tangled locks, with none of the sharpness of later combs. It was soft as silk on the head. Even after centuries of use there were traces of painting on the comb. I saw a beehive-shaped polished box, used to hold camphor for headaches, I think, for I remember one in childhood. There were carved wooden Welsh love-spoons, and a wooden candle-box. A tiny butter-print with a crest upon it probably once belonged to a child, for I had a small butter-print of my own by which my own small pat of butter was made. There were larger moulds, one with a cow, and another with sheaves of corn, and to me they were very familiar and loved objects, which seemed to carry the smell of the dairy, the freshness of new butter, the sight of a butter-churn, the coldness of spring water, and the shining smooth faces of those who worked at the butter-making. I bought a butter-print from the collection, with a carving of a bird, very beautifully cut deep in the wood. It was an old butter-print, probably early eighteenth century. I think the owners had kept it on the kitchen mantel-piece as a treasure, for the bird is decorative and stylised in design. Butter-prints were starting to go out of use in my youth, and 'Scotch Hands' were in favour as easier to work with and quicker with results, and they also gave the butter-maker a chance to indulge her own fancy in the pattern she used on the butter.

A BUCKINGHAMSHIRE LANE

The Buckinghamshire lane, with steep banks and slashed hedge on the top, and narrow road winding crookedly uphill and down, never very steep, is always interesting. Here white violets grow. I have seen the leaves in winter and in March I come to find them. It is difficult to spy the flowers, for the hedgerow seems to have a system of camouflage, a game of false clues which is spread out for one's discomfiture. First a little snail shell, like a curl of a petal, shaded with blue, snow-white in its curves, is picked up. Then a snowy pebble, and next bird droppings which are cunningly laid among the violet leaves, as if they are flowers.

But these things also are Spring's—
On banks by the roadside the grass
Long-dead that is greyer now
Than all the winter it was;

The shell of a little snail bleached
In the grass; chip of flint, and mite
Of chalk; and the small birds' dung
In splashes of purest white;

All the white things a man mistakes
For earliest violets
Who seeks through Winter's ruins
Something to pay Winter's debts.

Perhaps only in childhood one is not deceived by these scraps of pretence, for a child is so close to the bank, down near the earth. The violet's pale stalk, the snowy buds, the peeping hesitant flowers are visible to the quick eye and searching hands of a country infant. We used to walk along the hedges bent double, with sleek ribboned heads as low as our knees, as we crept along, seeking the treasures which we knew were there. We crouched, we crept, we tore holes in the knees of our long woollen stockings as we knelt on the sharp stones in the paths.

There, in the hedge banks we found the robin's nest, the wren's, the chaffinch's, hidden in the low forks of the nut trees, which made a barrier of branches and twigs, with crumbling soft earth between the roots.

LENT

Mothering Sunday is kept in the villages and daughters take flowers to their mothers, preferably white violets and celandines, arranged in some charming manner.

On Palm Sunday in Buckinghamshire figs were eaten and the day was called 'Fig Sunday'. Little crosses of palm, blessed at the altar, are given away at the church door on Palm Sunday here, and the church is decorated with palm willow, the gold-dusted sallow which grows in the lanes, the 'mealed-with-yellow' sallows for Palm Sunday of Gerard Hopkins.

During Lent the English Church uses the canticle 'Benedicite Omnia Opera', which is the most universal of all, and although nowadays the verses are telescoped several together, to shorten the long list, I wish we had each invocation separate, for this is to me the most poetical of anything in the service.

'O ye Winds of God, bless ye the Lord, praise him and magnify him forever,' we sing, and the North Wind and the South Wind and all the breezes, with the strong West Wind and the fierce East Wind, whistle and moan.

'O ye Fire and Heat, bless ye the Lord, praise him and magnify him forever'—and the kitchen fires and the bonfires crackle and send up their sparks to the sky.

MARCH

'O ye Ice and Snow, bless ye the Lord, praise him and magnify him forever,' and the vast Polar regions, the icebergs and the snow mountains, the snow in the sky, the ice on the earth, all praise the Lord.

This is the hymn of the elements, the paean of praise by Nature; the whole order of creation, including rain, frost, lightning and clouds, Sun, Moon and Star, are called to bless the Lord, with whales and all that move in the waters, with Fowls of the air, Beasts and Cattle, and everything in the Universe. Stars and spirits and souls, archangels, and among them Children of Men.

It always seems to me to be the greatest hymn of praise ever written. The world, spinning on its own axis, moving in its orbit round the sun, a part of the galaxy, aloof and cold and indifferent to man, is drawn into a living whole. The worship of God is not for man alone, but for the whole of creation. The link between man and nature, so badly broken by man, divorced and denied, is stressed, and strengthened. The supernatural is accepted by things animate and inanimate, and Nature herself is drawn into worship and praise with man on the same plane as plants and animals in that tremendous scale.

As we stand in the little church, under the heavy beams and queen posts of the fine roof, and sing, there seems to be a vast listening; stone carved heads of kings and bishops on the corbels, prick up their ears, the flat tombs with brass figures on the floor are aware, the trees outside in the churchyard, the woods and low hills on the horizon, the clouds and sun overhead take up the song of praise. It is their song, their music we sing today in Lent.

I am lost in the contemplation of this vast concourse outside the stone walls, stretching away to the ends of the Universe and I hardly understand anything else in the service.

'The speed of light is 186,000 miles a second,' I remember. I never forget this speed, whenever I hear of a plane slowly flying at 700 miles an hour. How many light-years away is the nearest star? The nebula in Orion's belt—is that Universe praising

God? Orion was known to Job. 'Canst thou bind the sweet influences of Pleiades, or loose the bands of Orion?'

So I ponder, standing with the congregation, kneeling mechanically, but lost in speculation, until I am roused by 'The peace of God which passeth all understanding', and the service is over.

I think of the astronomer monk, Father Cortie at Stony-hurst, whose work we followed with great interest. We visited the observatory and the distinguished scientist welcomed us and allowed us to gaze through the eyepiece of his great tele-scope. There was the noise of clockwork as the roof slowly revolved on the platform, to keep a slit opposite the telescope. We watched the image of the sun spots on the paper below the eyepiece, and I wished to stay there to work humbly as his assistant. We could see sun spots through a darkened glass with the naked eye, and to look at them through that great telescope was a new experience. Father Cortie was a household name in the small scientific set to which I belonged, his papers were read among us, and when he died I felt that a star had fallen from the sky.

A Glass Darkly

This early spring I had a discussion with Walter de la Mare about the Biblical phrase, 'Now we see through a glass, darkly, but then face to face' which I had always taken literally, as meaning the view through a window pane.

He, with his questing, imaginative mind, opened up many possibilities, the alternative readings for 'glass'. It might be a divining glass, a crystal in which we see future events, for such divinations were known in the east in those Biblical days. It might have been a mirror, reflecting the light, in which the vision was regarded, a polished metal surface held up to see behind the looker, such as the Roman ladies used for their toilet.

A landscape viewed through glass has a different texture from the scene regarded with the naked eye directly, and even the wearing of spectacles makes a difference, for it is not only that a portion of the light is absorbed by the glass, and a small part is reflected from the surface, but something stronger and more important is missing. When I travel by car with windows shut I feel cut off from the life around me, a space-traveller insulated from atmosphere, existing in a false vacuum. As soon as the window is dropped the trees and fields approach and share that elusive but deep warmth of living. We are face to face, we do not see through a glass darkly. It is not only light that is cut off, but other vibrations which affect us although we may not be physically aware of them, except subconsciously, neither ultra-violet light nor infra-red, but an interaction between ourselves and the world around us. There is a direct contact with nature as we breathe the air that has just swept against her body, we receive the light of the sun with no intervening screen except the atmosphere, we bask in a stream of closeness to reality, which has evaded us with the glass between. Even in a house, static and warm, we miss this meeting face to face. This is one of the differences between man and animal. We are used to glass houses, they perhaps see God in the eye of the sun, and the fingers of the trees and the body of the earth. They can bear the curtain of night, the brightness of stars, when we turn to the shelters we have built against these things, for we see through a glass darkly.

A First Taste of England

March 28th. A New Zealand farmer and his wife, newly arrived in England, strangers, came to see me, and I took them for a drive to get a first impression of English country, for this was their first visit to our land. It was a cold March day, and I feared the countryside would be dull to their eyes. No trees in leaf, no wild flowers except for the close seeking, but the bare branches of delicate colour were in the hedges, so that we could distinguish the wild rose by its pale green briars, the ash by its silvery sheen, the dogwood by its crimson as we speeded along the lanes, our heads turning to right and left, to absorb everything, cottages, inns, cattle, fields. We went along the narrow road with the signpost 'Little Hampden only', a lane I adore, for its majestic hedgerow trees, and its flowers in summer, and its air of welcome to me.

We went to the very small church of Little Hampden, but first we stood outside the porch to see the great curving timbers, and the small room, the bell-chamber, over the oak door. One rope hung down, to be pulled by my old friend, the bellringer, who has been the ringer and church cleaner for thirty years. We entered the little church, which only holds about thirty people, and the New Zealanders stood in the first English church they had seen. The altar is stone, a primitive plain table of stone, and the small pews are of oak. There are wall-paintings of the fourteenth century, and deep set windows, mostly of plain glass through which one can see the trees near by, and the farm below the road, and the distant hills.

Next to the church is a cottage, where a friend lives. The garden runs down parallel to the graveyard, and cottage, church and farm are alone in the lane here. Nobody answered when I knocked, so I lifted the latch and we peeped inside the door to see the white room with lovely china, lustre and Staffordshire mugs, the old jugs in a row on the long shelf over the fireplace, and the flowers on the table. My friend was not there, and we turned away. We had seen an old cottage and an ancient church, and we went on our way to see the first farm for my visitors.

We were welcomed by Miss Langston, who made the New Zealand farmer sit down in a corner of the curved settle by the fire. Over the fireplace were many horse brasses, most of which had been used on the family's own horses. One brass they admired was a design of a rose, a delicate piece of brasswork, and uncommon too. There were raying suns and horned moons, horses and pointed stars, such as we had in my childhood home, a score or two of these, each with a memory of the horse who had worn it. There were brass bells to stand up on the horse's head, to ring as he went proudly on, and the round 'ringers' to hang at his neck.

We stood for a minute at the gate of the farmyard to see the cattle and a white horse, and the mud from recent floods, and while we waited in contemplation of the magnificent trees in the centre of a great field, and the chestnuts on the lawn, and the lambs and sheep close to the farm buildings, Miss Langston found a small present for me. It was a root of the house leek growing on her roof, for me to plant on my own small house, as we had house leeks in my country home. It is a preservative from fire and lightning.

So now we had a farmhouse to add to our trophies of English country. Through woods and lanes we drove to Thame, for I wanted them to see a fine old market town with a broad High Street where the market is held. It was not market day, but the street was crowded with cars and vans, and busy people shopping from the villages. We looked at the Inn signs, the Fox, the Black Horse, the Spread Eagle, and across the road, the Bird Cage, the Elizabethan inn which hangs like a cage itself with its overlapping storeys.

Then along the Aylesbury road, and to the 'Bull's Head' for tea. This is a fourteenth century inn, in the market-place, with lovely staircase and a room where the yard used to be, so that the gallery which once looked down at the horses and coaches now is open to the room below.

It was time to go home, and we drove between well-layered hedges, newly plashed and sloping in delicate tracery of naked thorn branches, miles of newly layered hedges which interested the New Zealanders, for each length, cut by different hedge-cutters, was of a different pattern and had its own individual craftsmanship.

THE BORROWING DAYS

The last three days of March are said to be days borrowed from April and these have proverbially bad weather.

MARCH

March borrowed from April,
Three days and they were ill.
The one was sleet, the other was snow,
The third was the worst that e'er did blow.

and today at the end of the month, it is wild and windy, and in
Scotland there is snow.

The story of the borrowing is one told by parents to children
in past years, and the following is a version told by a nurse
eighty years ago, who heard the rhyme from her parents.

March said to Aperill,
'I spy three hogges on yonder hill.
And if you'll lend me dayes three
I'll find the way to make them dee.'

The first day it was wind and wet,
The second day was snow and sleet,
The third day it was sic a freeze,
It froze the birds' nebs to the trees.

But when the three days were past and gone
The three silly hogges came hirpling home.

These three days are the Blackthorn Winter, the cold spell at
the end of March and beginning of April when blackthorn is in
bud. This borrowing legend occurs too in France and Spain,
and people would not lend or borrow on these three days.

On March 31st a robin came into the kitchen. It sat first on a
geranium in the window, and then on the spout of the little
watering can. Three daffodils are out in the garden and blue
denticulata primulas.

APRIL

Who knocks? That April?
Lock the door!
I will not be pursued.

—EMILY DICKINSON

THE BLACKBIRD

The song of a blackbird comes every morning without fail,
wet or fine, from the gable-end above my open bedroom
window. It starts about 4 a.m. and I lie and listen, enchanted
and never tiring of this rhapsody. After about an hour the bird
goes away, and later it sings the same song, with different little
motifs in other parts of the garden. I have heard it practise a
short phrase, and then give it in full the next morning at dawn.
The song is the clearest, roundest and most delicious of any I
have heard from a blackbird, and I can recognise my bird's song
whether he is out in the fields, or in other gardens or woods near.

APRIL

Some of the cadences are his own invention, unique and exciting, and I wonder whether other birds are aware of this. I think they are, for there is a silence as he sings, as if others listened.

This amazing songster is distinctive in every way, and fearless, so that I can approach near him in the garden. I am half afraid for his lack of care, lest he should attract attention. He has a white cap on his head, as if it had been dipped in a flour barrel, and his feathers are very sleek, and his eye questing, as he looks in at the window in the daytime. He is the only albino I have seen around, and he is bolder than the other birds.

This is his song, and I swear these are his words, for I have often written down his phrases as he sings. The order varies and he repeats a phrase which he likes; he is proud of it. His voice is a countryman's, rich and rare.

> *Well, I'll be going.*
> *Kiss. Kiss. Kiss.*
> *I'll see ye tomorrow.*
> *I'll be going.*
> *What is't ye see'st?*
> *Tut! Tut!*
> *What are ye up to?*
> *Where are ye going?*
> *One. Two. Three.*
> *I'll see ye tomorrow, see?*

The lovely questions, the lilt at the end of each phrase, or sentence, the sudden ejaculations, the musical turn of the 'words', all repeated with variations and with repetitions now and then, make me lie awake in utter content.

At first I never saw the blackbird, as I was half asleep at dawn, but the voice was very near to me, and the song, or talk, as I imagined it, came in an intimate way, like a conversation of some celestial being. It spoke in broad Devonshire, I decided, a most warm and delightful Devonshire dialect, an alluring voice, to draw the soul out of one's body, so that I felt some kind of enchantment was up aloft. The sprite of a Devonshire countryman was talking to me and to all who wished to hear. I heard the same song in the garden later in the day, and spied my dawn singer, but often he goes to the gable at evening, and sings to the young moon.

Another blackbird has a different tale to tell, and again I know it anywhere, but it has none of the beauty of my white-headed blackbird's song. Nor does it answer my bird, or sing to it.

> *Where did ye go to?*
> *What did ye pay for your sausage?*
> *Where did ye get it?*
> *Oh. Oh. Oh.*
> *What have ye got, Boyee?*
> *What did ye pay for your dot, Boyee?*

This song is nonsensical in a serious materialistic world, and sausage is odd—but no other word fills the sound, and sausage it must be. On April 4th a strange blackbird was singing an hour or two at dawn. I counted 120 phrases one of which was: 'My little darling, will you come with me?'

The blackbirds live in the garden, except the white-headed one which lives beyond the hedge in some other place. It spends its time here, eats from the bird table and drinks from the trough. Sometimes eight birds are in the garden, four couples enjoying the feel of short grass under their toes, as they run and dance, and flirt their tails and bow and spread their wings on the soft springy turf of the new-cut lawn. Sometimes chase each other, with fierce intent. There are no cats to trouble them, and Macduff leaves biscuit in his dog dish for them to finish, standing aside to watch, and then looking at me to see if I also am enjoying the sight. They care nothing for him, and nearly touch his nose, as they dip their beaks into the food. My ears never have enough of their song, as my eyes never cease from looking at the various shades of new green in beech and oak and ash, in hornbeam and hazel, in apple and plum, in the garden wood. I think of the Somerset tale:

94

APRIL

Where be yon blackbird to?
Us know where he be!
Under yon Wurzle bush,
And us be after he.
He be chasing us all day,
Us be chasing he.

The country dialect of the blackbird is very striking to all who know country talk, and although the bird sometimes flutes, it often sings for an imaginative and quick ear to catch a word, to invoke a human voice. Yet never have I heard a round, rich intonation such as this white-headed blackbird uses, a voice to startle Robinson Crusoe on his island, and to lure a traveller on to fairyland.

On April 12th I could put my foot on nine daisies at once, so spring had come even before the cuckoo called. I still see little country children seeking groups of daisies to try this 'charm'.

FLOWERS IN APRIL

Early this month, almost as soon as the rain stopped, a little country girl went 'flowering' to seek for the first spring flowers along every hedge, and bank and secret place. She found the first white violets, not just one or two, but a company of them sprinkled in the hedgerows. She made two good-sized bunches and sent them to me as an Easter gift. Scented blue violets, which I never can find wild in this part of the county, and deep rose-pink violets were with them. These rosy violets are treasures, the flowers are the colour of strawberries and she discovered them growing in a remote field. They may have been strays, or sports from the wild ones, but the colour was clear and fresh with no trace of blue or white.

The beginning of April has brought the first brimstone butterfly, and I made a wish as I saw it on April 5th flying in a wavering, hesitating manner across the lawn to the rock garden when it dipped down to the Kaufmanniana tulips and sipped at them. It is in the same category as the first swallow, the first call of wood-dove, the first cuckoo. Once I saw three brimstones flying in Rider's Lane on February 28th, and I walked up this rough pathway with the three yellow 'primroses' dancing in the air before me for a long way.

GOOD FRIDAY

Good Friday was wet and cold, but I ate my hot-cross buns, small, pale and highly spiced for breakfast, and I thought of other days when our dairy had willow-pattern dishes piled with home-made buns, each marked with a deep cross in reverence; buns not to be cut with a knife, ready for everybody to have some through the day. There was no austerity about them, they were rich and sugary and spicy, freshly made on Good Friday eve. We sang: 'Hot-cross buns. Hot cross-buns. One a penny, two a penny, Hot-cross buns' till we were silenced.

On Good Friday we did not go to church, but we went primrosing and violeting; it was the custom. We carried a basket and a reel of black cotton, and we picked little tight bunches, tied them as we crouched on the steep slopes of the fields, and put them in the baskets. The icy winds blew up the hills, we were half frozen, the baskets were caught and blown away, and we rolled and tumbled after them. Some of the bunches were posted to a hospital in a great town, some went in the milk churns to the milk-dealer, to soften his heart perhaps, some were sent to church, and a few were kept for the four little glasses, in the four corners of the table on Easter Sunday.

'On Good Friday we went to church in the morning, then in the afternoon we went primrosing for Easter Sunday church decorations,' said a young Essex-born woman to me this Easter. 'Often we went paigling at Easter.'

I was glad to hear this old word 'paigle' for cowslip. Gerard speaks of 'paigles', and so does Parkinson. I prefer cowslip, with the oxlip, which grew among the cowslips, but paigle is a very old word of unknown origin.

APRIL

Kilvert in his diary refers to some traditions of his day. 'The millpond was full and I forgot to look at the sun in it to see if he was dancing as he is said to do on Easter morning.' It is interesting to realise that the reflection of the sun in water is to be observed, when a gentle breeze might make the sun dance, and give pleasure to a child eager for miracles.

He goes on with the country lore. 'It is well to hear the cuckoo for the first time on Easter Sunday morning. I loitered in the lane again gathering primroses where I could from among the thorn and bramble thickets, and along the brook banks. I tied my primroses up in five bunches. With these five bunches I made a primrose cross on the turf at the foot of the white marble cross.'

We may be sure he did not carry a reel of cotton, but he tied with the honoured green string—blades of grass. I remember once at Easter in Cornwall passing one of those wayside crosses far from any church or any habitation, graves or memorials of the unknown, and seeing laid there bunches of primroses, freshly gathered.

'It was an old saying that if you don't wear something new on Easter Day the crows will spoil everything you have on. Mrs. Chalmers tells me that if it is fine on Easter Sunday it is counted in Yorkshire a sign of a good harvest. If it rains before morning church is over, it is a sign of a bad harvest.'

We say:

If the sun shines on Easter Day,
It shines on Whitsunday likewise.

This Easter I sent a pair of Swiss carved ear-rings to a sick friend, and she replied: 'I shall wear them on Easter Sunday in bed, so that the crows will not peck me for having nothing new.'

So the superstition of Kilvert's day is still carried out nearly a hundred years later, but although everybody goes to church with something new, a new hat, a dress, gloves, on Easter

Sunday, I have never before heard of this strange attack of 'crows'.

The little church is decorated with daffodils from all the gardens round, and long sprays of yellow forsythia, which we have been warming in the house ready, and branches of golden-brown beech buds, and blackthorn in flower. The deep window-sills are lined with moss from the woods, and in these soft green cushions are posies of primroses and violets, like a Botticelli garden, blue and white and yellow on the emerald background. Children often take charge of the porch, and put the wild flowers there which they have gathered. On the long stone seats under the timbered porch roof are earthenware jugs of flowers and branches of sallow, falling in yellow fountains. The deep-set window, where usually there stands a jug of drinking water and two glasses for the 'Thirsty Wayfarer', is lined with thick moss, fresh and brilliant, with bunches of white violets inset. I think this little church has the loveliest decorations I have ever seen, partly because so many of the flowers are wild ones mingled with blossoming trees, and leaves and branches, and partly because the church has the simple background of white walls and dark oak seats and ancient furniture. Only on the altar are the conventional flowers, great white lilies, in brass vases, like a seventeenth century picture.

A village mother told me about the Easter present her young daughter had made for her. She lined a kitchen basin with moss, and made a thick ring of celandines around the edge, with a concentric circle of primulas from her small garden, in many colours, to fill the rest of the basin, and a blue crocus in the middle. This girl always follows the seasons with flowers, from 'Mothering Sunday' to Easter and Whitsuntide, to Harvest and Christmas. Some little children here once sent me tiny green baskets they had woven from grasses and rushes, and filled with primroses and violets, and in the centre they put a hen's egg.

I make Easter eggs for some of the little boys to eat on Easter Sunday morning. I put starry leaves and ferny wild carrot which is just showing in the hedges and primroses around the eggs, binding them with strands of wool. Then I boil them, in strong coffee for brown eggs, in cochineal for pink eggs and in spinach water for green ones. Everyone buys chocolate eggs, so these real eggs are different.

THE LILY

A friend from a village near my Buckinghamshire home is exiled in Canada, and she misses the English scene, the days of awakening spring, with the talk of the country people, as she looks out on snow from her air-tight flat in a great commercial town in Ontario. She writes to tell me of Easter in Canada.

On Good Friday the snow lay cold and soiled in the street outside, and no sun shone. Then a miracle happened. A knock came at her door, and when she opened it a tall and beautiful lily was there, in a flower-pot, left with no name. There was one perfect flower whose white petals turned back to reveal the gold, two flowers were gently opening, and three had tightly closed long buds. It was a personal visit of a flower, an Easter guest who entered, and she was moved to tears at the beauty in her homesickness, for she remembered a saying: 'Do not look for Him any longer in the tomb. Look for Him in the garden.'

On Easter Day at dawn the sun rose over the roofs opposite and under its glowing light the newly-fallen snow lay rose-pink. The lily now had three glorious trumpets fully formed and the light shone through them so that they became shining silver where the petals curled and a pattern of shadows lay within the calyx. The lily took on a rare mysticism of its own, it was a portent.

Each morning she came down at day-break to watch the light fill the glistening cups as the lily stood silently receiving the benediction of the new day. Then, passing through the streets during the following week she saw pots of lilies everywhere. In each shop window a lily was thrust among the goods displayed, and in the windows of the dwelling houses a lily stood. Some were sad lilies, in grim surroundings, but the lily is the emblem of Easter there as the Christmas tree is the symbol of Christmas here.

So the lily in the shop tries to find a little light as toys, cigarettes, hair-curlers and cheap hats press around it in the overcrowded windows, and it looks out with its innocent air between the heavy garish 'drapes', its flowers turning grey and drooping, without water in the stifling atmosphere of central heating. But, as Santa Claus in the gutter cannot spoil Christmas, so the debased lily cannot lose any of the glory of the Easter garden, and always it gives out a radiance and holiness.

The Annunciation is associated with the lily, and a pot of lilies is shown in a thirteenth century picture, between the Virgin Mary and the angel. This is one of the oldest examples of the lily theme, when the flower is shown, not as decoration but as a symbol.

In the Fra Filippo Lippi picture of the Annunciation the urn of lilies stands on a low wall, and Mary sits at the entrance to the room, the angel in the garden. Here the lilies are full of grace and beauty, their petals are unfurled and the gold stamens displayed, while some of the long narrow buds have the tips half-uncurled, pointing downward like fingers. It is this symbolism of the lily that has given rise to Easter decorations with lilies.

An April Day

Today I drove to the wood in the next valley to look for primroses. Part of the wood is preserved and a keeper wanders with his gun to warn and shoot any roaming dogs. As I sat on a tree stump with my little Scottie on his lead, I heard the sound of a gun, and fearful lest the man should mistake Macduff for a black hare or a badger, although he resembles a small black bear more than a poor frightened Wat, I stayed with him. The keeper came up and congratulated me on keeping my dog checked. I explained I had come to gather primroses, and I

APRIL

knew all about preserved woods from childhood days. We talked about badgers, he had seen a dozen badger holts in the woods not far away. We spoke of pheasants and their rearing, and many country topics. I left the small dog tied up to the tree, and gathered the early primroses which grew in tiny rosettes, very close to the ground, their stalks short and pink, their flowers small stars, as if they were all very new and innocent and surprised at looking out at the world.

Sometimes there were clumps of cowslips, in green bud, and here and there I found the leaves of coral root. I promised myself to come later, when the primroses are fully out and the coral root is in tall blossom.

The blackthorn covers the little crooked trees, the lime has its greeny flowers, and the wild cherry is in bud, some of it in flower, with never a leaf, the cherry blossom like tufts of snow fallen on the trees from the cold blue sky.

In the garden auriculas are in bloom, the 'Beares ears or French Cowslippe' of old days. I have yellow, purple and blue and murrey coloured, with tawny ones and a greenish and a white, all most delicate, delightful flowers. Why are auriculas so much more interesting than primulas? Perhaps it is the mealy leaf, for one name which we used in childhood, taught to us by an old woman we knew, was 'dusty miller'. Perhaps it is the strange colours, and the seeing eye of the flower. Thornton's prints of the auricula made me even more aware of these flowers which bordered many a cottage garden in my youth. 'They are not unfurnished with a pretty sweete sent,' says Parkinson.

I have taken slips of lavender and rosemary, and pushed them in with a prayer and a wish.

CUCKOO AND ROBIN

On April 15th, at six o'clock Summer Time, for we had put forward the clocks the day before, I lay half-sleeping, listening to the birds in the garden and wood, when I heard the round robust call of the cuckoo. It sounded near, and I had no doubt the cuckoo had come back to my garden. This call, the herald of spring, has always been most important to me, as to many country people. We used to listen for days, with ears pricked for that shout through the woods. Then we turned our money, and made our wishes, and purses were turned over in voluminous skirts, and coppers were jingled in men's pockets, and a sixpence was borrowed very quickly, to bring good luck.

So I got out of bed, and turned a shilling, and I made a confused wish, as I thought of various delights. The garden lay fresh and green with a film of frost over the grass-blades, and I stood at the open window looking for the bird who called again. Then I saw him in the tall beech tree, which he and his relations visit every year. He sat on a high thin bough, and bobbed and curtseyed, and called 'Cuckoo' to the world and to me. I was so near I could see his head as he turned this way and that. He seemed to be looking around at the changes from his high vantage post. There had been changes, too, for some new red-brick houses had been built near, and trees were cut down. I was glad that the tall beech tree was just the same, and the curving crest reared against the sky was ready for him.

Each year a cuckoo sits on the tip-top of the beech to look over the country. It can see for miles, over the red houses, far away to the woods of Penn and High Wycombe, but I think it was looking for a pair of elms across a field, for I have noticed that the cuckoos sing in my tree, and then fly across the road, to the tall fan-like trees in a hedge. Luckily they too had been left standing, and after about twenty minutes of contemplation, with occasional calls which were answered by two more cuckoos, the bird flew slowly towards the elms. It flapped its wings and bobbed and swayed before it started off, for the bough was slender, and all the time it sat there a gentle swaying of the branch made a see-saw for it.

The cuckoo flies fairly low, and it is easy to see his barred breast and grey wings as he soars heavily down from the beech wood across my lawn. It is his invisible highway in the air, a path he always takes. Before he sets off he has a long look round from his high tree; then he launches himself on the short journey over the road, for there are houses and cars and people where not long ago there were only fields. Each year he sees a difference in the landscape.

All the woods seemed to listen, every creature was filled with surprise at the suddenness of the call. An owl gave a long-drawn hoot—it lives somewhere near in the trees—and then a turtle dove began to coo, calling: 'Take two coos, Taffy! Take two coos, Taffy! Tak!' I was convinced that each bird was as surprised as I, and the odd silence that greeted the call, and then the songs of other birds coming fast, reminded me of the manner in which the nightingale is greeted.

At midday, when the sun was beating down, I walked in my small garden, and there among the daffodils I saw a round, white face and two large eyes regarding me. Something watched me approach, and I was startled by the intensity of the gaze. It was like a cat, but a very sinister large cat, and I went slowly towards it. Then, without a sound it rose in the air, spreading out brown flecked wings, and away it went, with the beautiful silent motion of the tawny owl. I was so astonished, I could only stand and stare, but the birds mobbed it and such a chatter and cry came from the wood the owl must have gone back to its nest. Rats may live in the banks of the daffodils, and I think the owl was helping to diminish them. Every night there is a great hooting and an owl sits in one of the trees near.

The robins are more numerous than ever. They come into the house, one at the back door and another at the french window, and they sing for food if it is not ready. One taps on the window at lunch time and asks for more. One straddles in the doorway and then flutters to Macduff's food bowl, with an eye on the Scottie. A robin has made a nest in the garage over the way.

The cuckoo certainly brought belated spring here, for the next day I saw the fat droning bumble-bee, and the first peacock butterfly, and a bat flew through the twilight air. I thought of the old story of the seven sleepers, who awake with the spring. 'The bat, the bee and the dormouse, the squirrel, the frog, the toad and the snake.'

The thrush sits in her nest close to the front door, and when the door is open she can see into the house. She peers out from her nest, and watches the goings-on, as rooms are swept and mats are beaten, and people come and go.

All these are the homely birds, they share the house and garden. The cuckoo in the tall beech tree, which he knows so well, his lighthouse, his gazebo, his attic window, and the robin who refuses to eat from the bird table but hops indoors for the crumbs on the kitchen table, because he likes company, and the thrush who sees everything from the postman to the visitor, and then the owl who calls in the garden, and knows more than I can say.

CUCKOO SONGS

We always welcomed the cuckoo in my childhood, with the short song:

> *Cuckoo. Cherry tree,*
> *Catch a bird and give it me,*

making a duet with the bird itself, so that the echoing cuckoo came after each phrase. The cuckoo seemed to be aware of the duet of call and answer, as it joined in with the human children.

In Cheshire we sang the well-known ditty:

> *The Cuckoo is a witty bird,*
> *He singeth as he flies,*
> *He bringeth us good tidings,*
> *He telleth us no lies.*

The word 'witty' has the old meaning 'cunning'. My little Cheshire maid came to me one day in great indignation. A man had tried to borrow our gardening shears, and she knew that he had borrowed them before and spoiled them. He used guile to get them again, and she had answered him back and sent him away. 'He was proper witty, but I was witty too,' she told me, triumphantly, her cheeks scarlet with the tussle.

> *The Cuckoo comes in April,*
> *He sings his song in May.*
> *In the middle of June he changes his tune,*
> *In July he flies away.*

Another version is:

> *In April come he will,*
> *In May he sings all day.*
> *In June changes his tune.*
> *In July prepares to fly.*
> *In August go he must.*

The Derbyshire rhyme runs thus:

> *The Cuckoo is a merry bird,*
> *She sings as she flies,*
> *She brings us good tidings,*
> *She tells us no lies.*
> *She sucks little birds' eggs,*
> *To keep her voice clear,*
> *That she may sing cuckoo,*
> *Three months of the year.*

The call of the cuckoo is said to be that of the male only, but this is still disputed. The female has a delicious call like water bubbling in a spring, and one can hear it every day.

I never tire of the cuckoo's call. I can hear it with pleasure for hours on end, for the two notes vary so enchantingly. There is nothing mechanical about that smooth romantic voice, and England without the cuckoo in spring would not be home for me. But townsmen living in the country point out that the cuckoo sings flat, that he is monotonous, that he is immoral. This is giving human attributes to a bird.

The cuckoo was identified with the coming of spring in my

country childhood, and old men and young welcomed the bird, whilst the women ran out to listen, to turn their money in their pockets and to make a wish. I joined in this hurry to hear the bird, and turned my own penny. The cuckoo was more than a symbol, he was spring itself, a mystery and a beauty, bringing the green to the trees, the flowers to the meadows, calling the fresh airs to the hills, for he proclaimed the eternity of youth and spring.

There have been many festivals associated with the cuckoo, and it was no sentimental idea to welcome the bird, but the relic of an ancient feeling about his coming. He was a visible and audible sign of the calendar, and when people had no almanacks and no printed words, he was the sign that spring had come. For a thousand years, two thousand years, the cuckoo's advent has meant spring, and so this old tradition has remained in country places, and it still exists, for here in Buckinghamshire village people listen and make their wish, as indeed do country men throughout England.

A letter from Walter de la Mare this April, when I wrote to tell of my cuckoo's arrival, says.

'How characteristic of that cuckoo to do his duty and his delight *for once*. Can you possibly tell me how it is the whole brood of them—cuckoos—are bound to be round about the 15th? And isn't it extraordinary how much loved by the people (even including the rich, I believe) are the birds which have earned it so queerly—not like you and me, almost solely for their beauty?'

The cuckoo calls, and is it to send out a message to his friends that he is here, or does he call in wanton joy at reaching his own beloved land, his fields and woods and individual trees? His two notes are so rich, so beautiful, I am enchanted and lost. Somebody speaking of bird song on the wireless, said he did not include the cuckoo in his songsters, as it was only a call. So the turtle dove's moan is only a call, and the nightingale's first tremulous note, that long drawn heart-shaking trill, is only a call!

APRIL

It is said that the interval between the two notes increases as the season advances. First it is a minor third, but at the end it is a perfect fifth. I often write down the calls in musical notation but I get no regularity of change, as birds differ. One cuckoo is very individual in his calling, as he seems to strive to get the correct interval. The cuckoo calls continuously in the early morning and I counted over 200 calls before I dropped to sleep again. I have heard over 500 calls with only a slight pause between making a short break. The blackbird's note is like a flute or recorder, the thrush is like an oboe, singing each air twice.

Cowslips

Cowslips are out in the meadows, under the hedges, and on the banks, but they are scarce in this part of Buckinghamshire, and I do not find as many as usual with new houses and ploughed fields. Nobody makes cowslip wine, that delicate and aromatic wine which is one of the most English of drinks. We picked the flowers from a cowslip field of our own, and a little band went out after breakfast with baskets and a clothes-basket. Each small basket was filled with the speckled flowers, and the contents dropped into the large clothes-basket which lay near. It was an occupation that delighted everyone, a freedom from the house, a day in the open field, among the lovely scented flowers. Cowslips are easy to gather, the stalk snaps with a click, and the flower heads are diverse, with their many bells. There was the excitement of looking for an oxlip which brought a wish to the lucky one, and the fascination of crouching close to the earth among the creatures that live there, the bees and ants and beetles, the scurrying frog, the hedgehog, the mole.

Two people carried home the clothes-basket when it was full, and at night the 'peeping' began. The yellow flower was pulled from the green calyx and stalk—this was the 'peep'. There were two heaps, the great piles of green which lay on a sheet, and the pile of yellow peeps, which filled the bowls.

The peeps were measured into the pancheon, and the receipt for the wine was eight pints of peeps, to eight of spring water, the juice and grated rind of two lemons, three pounds of loaf sugar, a sprig of borage, an ounce of yeast, and at the last a half-bottle of brandy. The boiling water was poured over the peeps, and the lemon juice and grated rind. This was left to infuse, but it was stirred daily. I remember the sight of this yellow pancheon on the stone bench, in the dairy, and anyone who entered that cold room gave it a stir with the long wooden spoon. After four or five days it was strained, and the sugar and yeast were added. It was poured into a stone jar to ferment, and after fermentation was over, in about three weeks, a half-bottle of brandy was added. It was bottled and put away in a dark passage. There it stayed for a year, to be brought out for visitors. There was an immense pride in the cowslip wine, and we were frugal of this golden liquor, which contained the cowslip bells of spring.

Lady's keys is a simple name, and we thought the flowers were like a bunch of my mother's keys which she kept in a horn cup. St. Peter's Herb is another name, after St. Peter's bunch of keys with which he unlocked the golden gate of Heaven. We sucked the cowslip bells for the honey within, as we walked through the fields, and we made cowslip balls and tossed them high in the air, letting the sweet scent fly round us.

We had a great love for cowslips, and we buried our faces in the bunches of flowers, absorbing the fragrance, trying to keep it for ever. We tucked cowslips in our straw hats, all round the crown in the white ribbon, like a fringe of little bells.

CANDIED FLOWERS

A friend came to see me this week in April, carrying a great bunch of cowslips from a meadow at Hambleden on the Thames. She candies cowslips to decorate her home-made cakes, and when I went to see her at Henley Vicarage, she brought from her pantry a christening cake with white icing and a circle of candied cowslips round the edge, golden and fresh as if newly picked.

Her method is similar to the old way of preserving flowers, using gum-arabic in water, dipping the flowers within, shaking them, and finally dipping in sugar, and drying on a string.

To make crystal flowers. 3 teaspoonfuls of gum-arabic, in crystal form (this is important). It is put in a bottle and covered with 3 tablespoonfuls of orange flower-water. Leave three days to dissolve, shaking it often. Use a small paint brush to cover the petals of the flowers, the calyx and all parts accurately. Then dredge lightly with castor sugar, and gently shake off the loose sugar. Dry in hot cupboard on paper and store in a box.

Daisies, cowslips, forget-me-nots, narcissi, all of these flowers were used to decorate the cakes I saw and tasted. They had a fairytale look, as if some magic had been at work to catch and crystallize the flowers.

MAY

A May Carol

The following May Day song was written down and sent to me by an old lady who learned it in her childhood, when children sang it at the doors on May Day. She was one of those who went round singing it, about eighty years ago.

This morning is the first of May,
'Tis here that we begin
To lead our lives in righteousness
For fear we die in sin.

For if we die in sin
The Lord will to us say
'You must leave off those wicked ways
And turn to the Lord again.'

MAY

So take a Bible in your hand
And read the chapters through
And when the great Day of Judgement comes
God will remember you.

The fields, the meadows are so green
As green as any leaves,
And our heavenly Father waters them
With His heavenly dew so sweet.

I have been travelling through the night,
And the best part of the day
And now I have returned
I have brought you a bunch of May.

A bunch of May, my dear, I say,
Before your door I stand,
It's nothing but a spray, it's well spread about
By the work of our Lord's hand.

Bring me a cup of your sweet cream
And a bowl of your brown beer,
And if I live to tarry in the town
I'll call another year.

I have a bag upon my arm,
Drawn up with a silken string,
And all I want is a little money
To line it well within.

The clock has struck, I must be gone,
No longer can I stay.
So ladies all both great and small,
I wish you a joyful May.

This is evidently an old carol preserved orally. The 'May-Day Garland' in the *Oxford Book of Carols* slightly resembles it, but there are only four verses of inferior quality to this quick-moving spirited Mayers' song.

MAY

May Day

On May Day the horses wore their rows of polished brasses, their bells and their checkered head bands, blue and white; their tails and manes were plaited with ribbons, even when they were only going to the village.

On May Day the cows were turned out from their winter quarters, and there was great rejoicing both in the animal world and the human. The doors were left open, the gates were fastened back, and the cows went diffidently, and then excitedly into the field, racing up and down when they found they were really free, rubbing their horns and flanks against trees they loved in familiar places, galloping with tails high, sometimes fighting to settle an old score. They ate the fresh, sweet grass, and drank from the troughs. Then they settled down to a feast.

At Knutsford in Cheshire I remember the May Day procession through the cobbled streets with a crowning of the May Queen on the Heath and dancing round the Maypole each year. This custom is still kept there, but the crowds of townspeople who come spoil it.

In Hone's *Everyday Book* there is mention of delightful customs for May Day. Girls from the villages came into the towns with garlands of flowers which they took from house to house, partly to show the flowers in bloom in the country, but also to get a few pence. A garland was made of two hoops, crossing one another vertically, and covered with flowers, cowslips and primroses, and streamers of coloured ribbons. The garland was fixed to a pole about five feet high by which it was carried. In each of the apertures between the hoops was placed a smartly dressed doll. This had perhaps a religious origin, a very ancient worship of the Goddess of Spring.

When I was about eleven years old, I walked in a May Day village procession, carrying a similar garland which my mother had made. The two crossing hoops were bound with ribbon and covered completely with flowers, with ribbons hanging from the summit, and a bunch of pinks like a top-knot. Some of the children had great bunches tied on broom sticks, and others had balls of flowers, and wreaths which they held in two hands like half hoops. Although we were excited and happy, our steps flagged with the flowers, the weight increased, and a straggling little company arrived at the hamlet which was our destination.

On May 2nd I drove to a market garden near Penn to buy auriculas of every colour I could find. I also chose some linums, and Iceland poppies (although it is late for these), and small azaleas. The grass has been mown, the many birds walk on the shorn turf. I was up at 5.30 out in the garden, stepping slowly and softly, to see the birds. The great trees were gilded in the rising sun, a marvellous sight, as this is the best time of the day, and three wood pigeons sat up aloft, with shining coloured feathers like some celestial birds. The grass was silver-green, the air was wine, and there was such a sparkle and richness I envied the birds who could sit so high enjoying the scene. For I am convinced they were really enjoying the morning light from their vantage post, just as a horse will stand at a gate and gaze across the country to see the view. I looked at the wood pigeons with my field glasses, and I marvelled at their beauty in this early sunlight, as they turned their heads and let the sun flow into their feathers.

THE JACK-IN-THE-GREEN

Mr. Bailey, who keeps the little antique shop, crowded with Staffordshire figures and copper and brass pans, is a country-man who was born in Buckinghamshire. When he was a child at Chesham, he used to see two chimney-sweeps on the first of May. They went round the villages as Jacks-in-the-Green. Their names were Uncle and Bohmer and everyone used these familiar titles for the famous sweeps.

All through the year they swept the chimneys of the great houses. They had gone up chimneys as little boys, learning the hard way to be master-sweeps, and now they were men of importance, respected and proud of their calling. They had a fast trotting little pony, and a nice little cart, and they drove with an air of reflected grandeur, along the roads, through the towns, to all the fine houses of the old and famous families.

They swept the many chimneys of beautiful Shardeloes, the seat of the Tyrwhitt-Drakes. Shardeloes stands on the hillside near Amersham, overlooking the valley and the lake which is ever changing because it is fed by the elusive river Misbourne. The great house is classical, remote and lovely above the slopes, a still-life of an eighteenth century painter. The crowd of chimneys were the property of the master-sweeps who looked after them. In one of the rooms Princess Elizabeth slept four hundred years ago, when she visited the town, and there was until recently a painted sign in honour of the occasion in the Crown Hotel.

After Shardeloes, they visited other large houses, Chenies, the home of the Russells, with the range of twisted and fluted Elizabethan chimneys; and perhaps Latimer House and Penn House. There were many sooty chimneys in each house, and the master-sweeps were in command. Lesser sweeps swept the chimneys of smaller houses, and the cottagers swept their own with furze brush and boughs of juniper tied to a stick, and inserted up the chimney, or dropped down from the roof. Never must holly be used for sweeping a chimney, for holly is a 'gentle' tree, with traditions of the 'gentles' or fairies, and those who use holly offend the gods, and get bad luck. There is a tale of a poltergeist which came to a farm where holly had swept the chimney. It is a 'holy tree', too, from its Christmas connections.

On May Day the two men came round, each in his bower of green leaves, to dance. They wore wooden hoops, of diminishing sizes. Upon this framework boughs of bay and box, holly and ivy were fastened, and the top knot was a bunch of ribbons. In and out of the crowd they pirouetted, frightening the children, amusing the grown-ups, disporting themselves in carnival spirit. The man inside the bower of green was invisible, except for his feet, and his twisting and turning must have been like a great green top, spinning among the people.

MAY

Several country people have told me that they saw the Jack-in-the-Green in their childhood, and the custom of sweeps dancing entirely enclosed in a leafy garment has a tradition going back to before 1800. However the Jack-in-the-Green may be connected with the Green Man, and the strange carved heads of men with oak leaves, acorns and sprays of green, coming from their mouths, which decorate many of the old churches. In a fourteenth century misericordia at Lincoln Cathedral there is a striking carving of a Green Man who holds double acorns by their short stalks in his mouth. The origin of the Green Man is unknown, and I would like to see a collection of pictures of these corbels, which are some of the most fascinating in the churches of this country.

The chimney-sweeps' brushes always bring to my mind the tiny dark field-rush. It was one of the first signs of spring, and we knelt down to pick it, as it came out with the early primroses and the small cowslips and the wood anemones on the steep slopes of our favourite field. It was called the 'chimney-sweeper' and it was used, we imagined, to sweep the minute chimneys underground of some fairy inhabitants of the earth itself.

> *Golden lads and lasses must*
> *Like chimney-sweepers come to dust*

is the epitaph of those valiant chimney-sweepers, Uncle and Bohmer, in their little cart with the high-stepping pony, roaring along the narrow lanes of the countryside of Buckinghamshire to the chimneys of the rich and golden lads and lasses.

INTERLUDE

On May 5th I gave an address on 'Reading and Books' to some members of the Mothers' Union, in a newly-built area of this Buckinghamshire town. At the end, as I prepared to leave, three little boys entered the church-hall, seeking their mothers who were chatting to their neighbours. They were very little boys who stamped about and stared with interest at the gathering. So I stooped down and asked them, softly and privately, what they would like me to write about. If they could choose, what kind of tale would they wish for?

Two boys were shy and embarrassed, but the third was eager to tell me. He answered: 'About a poor man who gets rich.'

They all stared at me, pondering this exciting prospect of wealth, and I hesitated a moment, disappointed by the greed for money which had suddenly appeared in this infant's mind. Had he heard tales of men winning the pool, and getting a fortune? Was he already obsessed by the lure of gambling?

'I know a tale about a poor man who got rich. Shall I tell you?' added the little boy, so I listened. He spoke rapidly in so low a whisper I had to bend down and let him speak close to my face. We were all alone, isolated from the others as he told his tale.

'A poor man and his wife had no children,' he began. 'They were ever so poor. They wanted a baby, and at last a little girl was born. So they shut their house and set off with her. Her name was Peachling.'

'Peachling?' I asked.

'Yes, because she came out of a peach stone,' said he solemnly. For some reason my heart was immediately lightened, I felt as gay as a troubadour, as the little boy went on with the tale. The family arrived at a barn where they were going to sleep for the night. They lay down in the hay, father, mother and Peachling. In the dead of night robbers appeared with money which they counted. For some reason, which I did not grasp, the robbers were scared by the little family, and they fled leaving all their wealth behind. The poor man and his wife and Peachling were left with the gold. So the poor man became rich.

All this was whispered very secretly, urgently with intense concentration, by the tiny fair-haired boy.

I went away strangely uplifted. Nobody had heard a word, and I was the sole sharer of this ancient story, told in a little Mission church-hall, in the midst of all the new council houses, while the mothers gossiped about washing-machines and television.

MAY

There is an old magic about nuts and kernels, and perhaps the nomads in the deserts told these tales round the fires. A girl born from a peach stone, a chariot made from a walnut shell, a workbox fashioned from a nut, a golden ball-gown hidden in a kernel. A literature on this subject could be written, a piece of research on the essential beauty of this secret of the nutshell.

MAY WEATHER

There are fourteen cold days in May, say the country people. This agrees with another saying: 'Expect no summer before the thirteenth of May' and the old Buckinghamshire prophecy: 'As many mistises in March, so many frostises in May.' In this last saying the date of the mist or fog in March is the same as the date of the frost in May.

On May 14th, a country woman remarked to me: 'We are not going to be sure about frosts till May 17th is past. That was the date of the bad frost a few years ago when everyone was caught.' Thus dates are remembered and traditions are made, for that frost caught the new potatoes in thousands of little gardens. It ruined fruit buds and early plants, so it has been put on the black list.

On May 11th, 1872, Kilvert tells of the cold weather. 'This is the bitterest, bleakest May I ever saw and I have seen some bad ones. May is usually the worst and coldest month in the year but this beats them all and out-herods Herod. A black bitter wind violently and piercingly drove from the East with showers of snow. The hawthorn bushes are white with may and snow at the same time.'

CHURCH FESTIVALS

The day before Whitsunday I walked through the beech woods and across the fields to gather flowers. Cowslips were out in the meadows, and some of them were heavy with bells, twelve florets hanging from a stalk. Under the hedges grew the tallest flowers, with long brittle stalks, but every family of cowslips was rich in colour and scent this day of sweetness and blue sky and young green beech leaves. My companion was a schoolgirl, and she knew where the blackbird's nest was hidden and she showed me many a secret country thing.

On Whitsunday the little church at Penn was like a flowery dell with wild cherry blossom. The cherry trees grow in the woods, and many a wild cherry snowy with flowers rears its head among the beech trees. A wild cherry grows in my own little wood, and others are in the neighbourhood, dropping their petals like snow when a wind blows. Fountains of cherry sprayed over the steps to the chancel, and cherry blossom decorated the pulpit, with red tulips gleaming in the garlands of white. Red and white are the colours for Whitsuntide. The altar was flanked by stone jars, filled with wild cherry blossom, and I thought it might have been Cherry Sunday, a tribute to the orchards where the fruit is grown for the markets.

The church bells chimed down the valleys, and my young companion of the day before was one of the bell-ringers. The five girls and a solitary man can be seen pulling the bell-ropes in the tower, laughing and giving a word of advice to one another. Then with the last lone bell, they hurry to their places in the latched pews.

The next Sunday, Trinity Sunday, the cherry blossom had gone, but another harvest of wild flowers was brought to make the old church even more beautiful. It was Queen Anne's Lace, the wild parsley of the hedge banks. This lovely spraying flower was at its best inside a church, where, against the dark wood, it resembled the lace of its name.

It filled many jam-pots, hidden under the foam of green and white, which flowed up on the window sills, by the pulpit and about the leaden font. The scent of it was that of a country lane, and again I felt how fitting it was that a small country church should be decorated with the flowers of the fields and trees and hedges.

This is the month of great beauty in the windy flower-sprinkled Chiltern hills, blue as speedwell in the distance, the cherry orchards whiter than snow in the villages, and the great woods of beech trees, silver and delicate green, with violet-coloured shadows. The fields have cowslips, which grow they say where the nightingale sings, the lanes have traveller's joy and spindle trees and dogwood, with white violets on the banks.

In a garden in the town here a great old magnolia holds up a thousand cups, purple and white, and the bees hum as they sip from those thick fragrant flowers. I carried home some branches, but I was told that the magnolia's next-door neighbour complained of all the flowers hanging over the high red brick wall which divided the gardens. She asked for the tree to be cut back. So there can be too much even of beauty itself.

BUTCHER'S BROOM

May 7th. I went to a favourite little wood to look for periwinkle. The leaves which cover the ground under the beech trees have blue-green shadows, and the periwinkle flowers are the same colour, so it is difficult to see them. A glitter of light and shade fills the wood, filtering through the young beech leaves, and the evergreen periwinkle leaves with their strong reflecting surface send back this light in a thousand points, so that a dazzling underwater effect is produced in the wood.

Near it I found a bush of butcher's broom, which fascinated me, with its odd prickly leaves and minute flowers. The plants were once used to scour butchers' tables. In another part were bluebells and some white bluebells among them over which I made a wish. Forget-me-nots, and woodruff and sainfoin grew in the paths near, and blue and white milkwort, the first of the year.

MAY BLOSSOM

It was very unlucky to bring may blossom into the house, and I was never allowed to do this, nor was anyone in my childhood.

The smell of may blossom is sweet, but when the scent is very heavy under a great may tree, there is an odour of corruption. The solemn warnings of death were so serious, the severity of glances, as the branches of may were taken from me, were so compelling I never ventured to carry any indoors. Even now when I pick the lovely boughs, I put them in a jampot outside, to adorn a garden table or a corner of the porch.

Hawthorns were some of our favourite trees. They were magical, partly because of this warning, and also for some occult reason, some ancient folk memory of fairies. Their twisted old trunks, their dwarf size, their extreme beauty as they made a house of scented blossom, their ancient legends make them tabernacles of gods. The young green leaves, delicious to eat, were called 'bread and cheese'. The crimson berries, also very good to eat, for they tasted of bread, were called 'aiges' or 'aegs'. This is the old name, preserved in country places. It is the Saxon Haeg, which later became Hawgh and the Haw, but with us it kept its old name, which was often aspirated.

Hawthorns were not cut down, and when I heard of the fairy hawthorns in Ireland, I felt that I had always known the reason why. They were not struck by lightning, they were shelter for sheep, and they were very ancient, as they grew in rough stony pastures on the hills, which could never be ploughed.

NIGHTINGALE

On May 17th I heard the nightingale about 7 p.m. in a coppice. For some years nightingales sang close to my house and I heard them every night and day too, but they have been frightened away by new houses and their favourite bushes have been cut down. The sky was stormy, rain was falling, and the sun shining, so that strange blue lights appeared over the land-scape like the stormy scene in a Jan Brueghel picture. Then a double rainbow appeared. I realise that the great painter caught these transcendent moments of beauty and pinned them down for eternity. It is at these rare times of intense emotion in the atmosphere that a Brueghel comes to life again, and one sees what the Flemish artist saw, whether snow or evening light, or sunlight through a cloud.

HERBS

The rosemary bush at the end of the garden under the wood is in flower, and because this straggling bush is sheltered by the trees, and bathed in every ray of sunshine that comes in spring, it carries its lavender blue flowers a month or two earlier than any other rosemary here.

'Divers sweet gaping flowers, of a pale or bleak blewish colour, many set together, standing in whitish huskes,' says Parkinson in *Paradisi in Sole*.

It is a herb in general use, and I run up the grass, wearing my apron, to pick a spray for cooking, and on the way back I gather a bunch of parsley, and some thyme and marjoram. A sprig may enter a bouquet garni, with parsley, thyme, and a leaf from the little bay trees, the descendants of my Cheshire bay. It may flavour a stew, or lie in the roasting-pan under the meat.

It is said that rosemary came to the west brought by the crusaders from the Holy Land, and as it grows easily from slips inserted in the soil in spring, it is a herb everyone knows and loves. We used to put a small spray of rosemary leaves in pork and rabbit pies in the winter months when we had this farm-house fare, and into herb puddings when these accompanied boiled beef. Yet its evocative scent does not bring food to the memory but more serious things. The long sprays were twined in the wreaths for the dead, around the moss-covered willow which made the foundation. In the rosemary chinks the stems of roses, or snowdrops, or pinks were thrust according to the season. 'Rosemary for remembrance,' we said, and we gave rosemary for parting gifts to friends and relatives. Parkinson speaks of the universality of the plant in his day in the

'Woman's garden', and it is good to hear of a woman's own garden.

'This common Rosemary is so well known through all our Land, being in every woman's garden, that it were sufficient but to name it as an ornament among other sweete herbes and flowers in our Garden, seeing every one can describe it, but that I may say something of it. It is well observed as well in this our Land (where it hath been planted in Nobelmans and great mens gardens against the brick walls, and there continued long) as beyond the Seas, in the natural places where it groweth. . . .'

He speaks highly of its virtues. 'Rosemary is almost of as great use as Bayes, or any other herbs both for inward and outward remedies, and as well for civil as physicall purposes. Inwardly for the head and heart; outwardly for the sinews and joynts; for civill uses, as all doe know, at weddings, funerals, etc., or bestrow among friends; and the physical are so many, that you might bee as well tyred in the reading as I to the writing, if I should set down all that might be said of it.'

Sweet Cicely, sage, thyme, balm, basil, bay, tarragon, marjoram, parsley and rosemary were the usual herbs grown in country gardens, with rue for herbal medicines and camomile for camomile tea. I had a great bush of rue in a corner of this garden, but after many years of strength and beauty, it was caught last year in a prolonged frost and killed. The grey green leaves, so bitter to the taste, were decorative among flowers, and they gave out their own medicinal astringent odour, which is clean and refreshing. I picked the sprays of rue in May to put in the vases, with flowers, and its presence kept them fresh.

Why did Ophelia call it Herb o' Grace on Sundays? There have been several reasons proposed, but I think it was simply the clean, almost sanitary smell, which would refresh the air of a stuffy church and much-clothed congregation in Tudor days. Often we have taken a pinch of rue, shut it in the Prayer Book and gone off to church with the ferny leaves pressed and aromatic. Like Lad's Love or Old Man, (the names for Southernwood), the rue could revive an aching head and throbbing eyes with its fresh clean tang, cold as water, smelling like a bottle of smelling salts.

Old countrywomen, who were wise in the lore of herbs, used to make sandwiches of bread and butter with a chopped leaf of rue between, and this they ate at tea-time in the spring to give themselves an appetite, for a tonic medicine cost money.

One day I gathered a ferny leaf of rue and made a most delicate sandwich, but the bitterness remained for several hours to remind me of the strength of mind of those old herbal women who could sit down and eat a plateful of these.

It also brings to memory the rue-tea, made in a brown jug of antique shape, the earthenware sides decorated with a pattern of stylised leaves and crosses, the dark lid hanging by a string through two small holes. We had to drink half a cupful of this nauseous brew each morning, and no tears or struggles availed against the decree. The only hope of escape was the forgetfulness of the busy household, when in the flurry of milkcans and horses, of trains to catch and calves to be suckled, the minor ailments of children were forgotten.

Sage grows by the garden door, in a shady corner, although it likes the sun, and I give bunches to the wood-woman who likes roast pork for dinner. Thyme spreads in many corners, close to the ground, all ready for picking. Balm is too rampant, and it is often banished, but it comes up again, and it is used to flavour fish. The little bay trees are used every day, winter and summer, and their branches appear even in Christmas decorations. Tarragon is not very happy, it dies each year, and fennel grows so wildly I have to uproot it. Sweet marjoram is a spreader, and this too has to be torn up with its purple flowers, for it covers too much ground. Animals like sweet marjoram, and I discover frogs, toads and other creatures hiding there in the scented spikes. Parsley is the most common of herbs, and still I think it is the best, for it has green leaves throughout the year, and even in snow and frost it is good-tempered. I put in seeds in April, on a stony bed, for the roots like gravel, and they thrive there. Parsley, of course, must never be transplanted. It is an ill omen to give away a root. Chives grow in thick clumps, often forgotten, until the purple heads are in blossom. Mint is a ramping weed, but its smell is so delicious and cool, I never have too much. There are three varieties, one of them being lamb's mint. The leaf is large, deeply veined and slightly hairy, a lovely plant which is about thirty years old.

There are many herbs which I do not grow because I have not room for them, but often I gather the wild variety and drop it in the cooking pan; wild thyme, wild chervil, young nettles and young dock—the latter for salads. I walk through the woods with my fingers aromatic with the lovely grey-green wild wormwood, mugwort, and I strip it and sniff its cool fragrance as I go on my way.

THE LILY-OF-THE-VALLEY

My garden is the haunt of lily-of-the-valley, a flower which has been a favourite since childhood when we found it growing wild in the woods near my home. It grew there in vast quantities, for those were the days when people did not root up plants and take them away. The servant boy climbed the high ridge and picked a bunch for my mother when he returned from his day off. We went with baskets to gather the flowers once a year, and we arranged them with the small pearls in the centre and the long pale green leaves outside like a guarding fringe. That was the correct way to have lilies, the Victorian way. It was a 'bouquet', a traditional bunch.

In Cheshire, in Wales, and even in Buckinghamshire I tried in vain to make lilies feel at home. They refused to grow, they sent up a leaf or two and then disappeared. Then, for no reason they took root in my garden, and decided to stay here. The flowers fill a bed, they have pushed out the roses, they have hidden the little cyclamen and the primulas and the auriculas, and they have taken possession. They spring up in the gravel path, and they push their green spires into the lawn itself, to be mown down each week. They travel underground to rise up in other flower beds. There is no stopping them, for although I uprooted a quantity, they spread the faster. They are said to go to the east, so I move them to the west and let them travel eastward towards the rising sun.

'If you leave your door open, they'll go on and grow in the house,' my old gardener warned me. So I keep the door shut.

They have filled two flower beds, and part of another. They are springing up by the heap of coal, and wandering under the hedge to the rough orchard next door. They are quite at home, they are completely happy, because there is little sun in the path they have taken. Now I can grow them and enjoy the sweet fragrance which filled those lily woods. The flowers after their struggle for survival are very large, with fourteen bells on each thick stem, and a rare beauty. They grow so thickly that I can fill every bowl and vase with them, and at Whitsuntide they are the decoration of the house, when masses of white lilies scent the rooms.

Lilies-of-the-valley were the Victorian and Edwardian flower; they grew in every cottage garden, spreading by the hedges, and in the dark corners. Children took them to school in little bunches with two or three leaves at the back, to show up the pale white bells. They were much smaller than the lilies here, and very precious. The guard and the station-master wore nosegays of lilies-of-the-valley in their buttonholes in May.

I had a small green washbasin and jug with bunches of lilies patterned on the china, and I admired it as I washed myself. We had black papier mâché boxes with lilies on the lids, and little china pomatum pots and trinket sets with bunches of the flowers. The fashion for these lilies has not changed, and there is lily-of-the-valley cretonne, and lily-of-the-valley perfume in the shops. The Piccadilly flower shops are decorated with these flowers in May. Women sell bunches in the London streets, with violets. The Paris markets sell bunches arranged in the old way with the long pointed leaves surrounding the pearly bells in the centre, which is perhaps the prettiest way to display the lovely scented flowers. I feel happy that these lilies have come to my garden, to grow on the north bed where nothing else would grow, and I cannot grudge them the space they take as they overrun the flower beds and creep under the paths to take more possession. Perhaps I shall let them displace the other flowers and have their own way completely to enter the house and live here with me. They are not encouraged, they are not fed by any stimulant, they are not watered in droughts, they grow rampantly, but I am honoured by their presence. They are moving onward, an army of green, silently invading, and they provide cover for small creatures; a toad lives there under the long leaves, and field mice and frogs.

Lilies-of-the-valley grow wild in the woods of Gloucestershire, not far from the Roman villa at Chedworth and I hope to see them some day in the month of May.

> *They are the pearls of the earth. I ever knew*
> *In woods of my adolescence how fresh they grew.*
> *They are but loosely strung*
> *On green pale threads the warm May woods among.*

A Deserted Orchard

May 15th. We walked along a rough little Buckinghamshire lane this afternoon, to look for anything we could find. Stitchwort, which the children here call shirt buttons, grew in lacy patches, a needlework flower, from its names and from its embroidered edges and its slim flax-like stalks and leaves. Somebody might once have used the stalks in her fine needle to stitch a leafy garment together. Bluebells were hanging their bells on the banks, with a barrier of nettles near the cottages, and yellow archangel was out. Sheep and lambs grazed in one of the large orchards above the deep lane, and men had slashed the thick overhanging hedge in one place, where perhaps many birds had already nested. Forget-me-nots, woodruff and sainfoin grow on the banks and blue and purple milkwort, the first of the year.

My Scottie and I left the lane and crossed a large field which slopes steeply down to a valley and then rises just as steeply to a wood at the far side. I wandered about looking for late cowslips in the thick grass, and then I entered the deserted orchard at the top of the opposite slope. Old apple trees were laden with blossom, cherry trees had dropped their petals and I gathered some straggling dipping sprays of pink apple flowers, which touched my face. This orchard of half-wild trees is haunted for me, and I always think of a farm which once stood there. Only the deep well and the aged apple trees and cherry trees are left to remind us of the past.

I carried the apple boughs away to decorate my long room, and I realised that only two days previously I had refused to accept some pink apple blossom from a Cotswold orchard, because, said I, 'It is unlucky to pick apple blossom.' This pious legend is firmly implanted on my mind, but my friends regarded me with suspicion. Country people made these taboos very often to preserve a decency. It was unlucky to gather apple blossom because the fruit would be lost to man, in those times when there were few imports and the produce of the country was very important. It was wasteful to destroy orchard fruit for a whim of beauty, and apple blossom must not be picked. The wild apple trees, the crab apples, the wild plums and damsons, the wild cherry and sloe could be gathered with impunity but the orchard trees were safe from pilfering hands.

ROBIN'S ADVENTURE

My daily help feeds a robin every morning at seven o'clock in her cottage, when she and her husband have breakfast in the kitchen. She puts scraps of bread and bacon just inside the open door which leads to the garden. The robin hops into the room and eats the feast. He waits on a tree and enters each day when the door opens. For some months this has been the daily arrangement of robin and human beings. Last week, the second week in May, as the robin fed on the floor, and the husband and wife sat at breakfast, a kestrel swooped through the open door, diving close to the heads of the man and woman who hit out in alarm at the bird. Somehow the robin escaped among the furniture, as the kestrel flew up and down seeking it. They could have caught the kestrel in their hands, but they tried to move it away to the window or out through the door. They were horrified at the speed of the attack, and the commotion of wings in their tiny kitchen. Peace was transformed into war in a twinkling, as the bird swept furiously about. Then the kestrel flew out through the door and away. They rescued the robin who was hiding, very frightened, but none the worse. I have never heard of an incident like this, an attack with people in the room, but I remember a priest telling of an owl which came into his room in the middle of the night after a budgerigar in a cage.

COBAEA SCANDENS

May 21st. The cobaea scandens, which is the only survivor from my amateurish sowing of the seed in a plant pot, is growing so fast I put a short stick near it, to which it now clings. I put a taller one, a few inches away, and I was amazed to see the plant actually move over an inch with sudden jerks. I stood watching, and it stretched towards the stick, and the tendrils are already reaching and clinging in ten minutes' time. The tendrils clasp the second stick and the plant is twined there. Next I placed a third stick, much taller, in the same flowerpot, about three inches from a leaf which has tendrils at its end. The leaf is slowly but visibly raising itself towards this stick. There is a slow motion and then sudden jerks. I saw a vibration in the plant and a jerk within two minutes of putting the stick in place. It is an uncanny sight, this visibility of plant motion, which one can see in a film, but seldom in reality. The iris stylosa comes out in water in the house in January from the close-furled buds, taking about an hour to uncurl. The movement of the cobaea scandens jerking to find the stick is different, it is almost disconcerting in its speed. I shall plant it in the garden in a week or two when there is no danger of frosts, and give it room to climb, for it already reaches the top of the window in the kitchen.

WORDS

I heard a new word this month of May, a word which seems to be confined to this part of Buckinghamshire. It is 'doufting' or 'dowftling'. It means paddling, and the children of Chesham in my country friend's youth used to go doufting in the brooks at Chesham—not paddling.

He used the name 'wag-wanton' for trembling grass, or quaking grass, as we called it, but this is well known and used all over the county and elsewhere. A London waitress, as I had lunch one day, told me she used to pick wag-wantons in her Essex childhood.

The word 'wick', meaning alive, a variant of 'quick' perhaps, is still used in Lancashire although I have not heard it elsewhere. A Lancashire friend told me that a child exclaimed: 'There's something wick on your sleeve' and there, creeping along, was a caterpillar. 'As wick as a weasel' is a vivid simile, which matches our childhood comparison 'As fause as a fox' or 'As tricky as a ferret'.

This friend spoke of an incident in the County School near Preston. The inspector examining the school was delighted with the drawings done by a little boy. He particularly liked a sketch of the gates of the Squire's lodge. He pointed out, however, that 'drawn from Nature' was incorrect when applied to sketching a gate.

'Can you tell me, boys, why these gates should not be described as "drawn from Nature"?' he asked.

'Because, sir,' answered a boy, 'Nature's wick.'

SMALL THINGS

As I walk through the woods and along the lanes, where the lane is narrow enough to exclude motor traffic, I soon lose myself in the wonder of country things, time slips into eternity, as one discovers the small things which make up country life. There is a rotten tree trunk with that white powdery wood called 'touch-wood', which we gathered to try to make fires without matches. Touch-wood would be very useful on a desert island, we thought, and we had only to hold a burning glass, to focus the sun's rays on it, and a fire would spring up. So we made little fires in the corner of the stones.

The earth is soft and yellowish, sticky and slippery, and there we could gather the clay, for clay is very good for making models, for fashioning into marbles and five-stones and baskets and leaves. It is useful for stopping pipes and making dams in narrow streams. So clay would be taken.

On the hills water comes from springs, rising up from the interior of the rocky earth. In the valley water comes from wells collected from the springs and lying in the green moss-covered rounded stones.

Perhaps we should find a spring, curving up from a damp patch in a field, which nobody would notice who was unused to a country spring. It is so small, so hidden, this tiny little fountain, but it is there, singing to itself a well-known earth song, as it trickles away.

There is a squeaking gate, an individual gate, a musical gate, and two trees are rubbing together to make a strange sound of high notes. Music is everywhere, waiting for the musician to find it. There is no loneliness, no dead silence, one is never alone, for the company of birds and insects and animals is present, invisible, but watching with many eyes.

OAK APPLE DAY

May 29th is Oak apple day, the date when King Charles II hid in an oak tree unseen by the soldiers. It was a memorial day, a triumphal day for England, and the anniversary was kept with the utmost vigour by people in my childhood. Every little boy and girl, every man wore a buttonhole of young oak leaves. It was essential that the date should not be forgotten, and there were dire penalties for those (and I was often one of the offenders) who forgot. So when I turned up in the playground on May 29th with no bunch of oak leaves I was punished. The luckless ones who had forgotten their oak received the penalty from eager hands thrust out with bunches of nettles. Wrists and fingers were lashed with nettle whips, and red places and white spots rose on the skin. It was very painful, and we fled to find some oak trees, or we rushed to the banks to gather dock to soothe the inflammation.

'Out nettle! In dock!' we cried, as we rubbed the spots.

At twelve o'clock one was free and could not be stung.

Kilvert was in London on Oak apple day in 1870, and he mentions in his diary that the porters at Paddington wore oak sprays in honour of the day.

I never saw anyone wear the oak leaves after my country childhood days, when everyone was on the side of King Charles, and we played Cavaliers and Roundheads. The curious thing about the wearing of the oak leaves was that we never talked of King Charles's escape. It was Oak apple day as important as a Saint's day, as Midsummer Day, as April Fool's Day, a worship of the oak tree, which was loved and feared in our superstitious hearts.

Never stand under an oak in a thunderstorm or you may be struck dead, they said, and we fled from oaks as if they were steel rods when, as often happened, we were caught in lightning and thunder. Animals sheltering under oaks were killed, and we lost some ourselves and heard of many others. Oaks struck by lightning were called 'blasted oaks' afterwards, and I remember seeing boughs and dead trees. So perhaps this wearing of the oak was a small tribute to the oak and its inimical powers, as well as to King Charles II.

JUNE

The first of June was spent on the rocky 'islet' at Tintagel, the traditional birthplace of King Arthur. I wandered idly through the little cells of the Celtic monastery, excavated ruins, on the rocky slopes of the cliff; little green rooms of fairy-tale houses, with walls a foot high of yellow bird's foot trefoil, and cushions of sea pinks, and tapestries of white sea-campion. Nature has taken over the furnishings of these ancient places. The scent of the island is ravishing but elusive, delicate but all pervading. It is sweeter than a perfume shop, it is soft and gentle as the breeze wafts it from the myriad flowers. Single flowers seem to have no fragrance, but the island slopes which are smothered in small waving petals, give out this aromatic smell.

The rocks of the island are carved in fantastic shapes by the wild weather and the buffeting they get from the Atlantic gales. There are pinnacles and towerlets, and castles and halls of demons. In the ledges and round holes and hiding places of these stone sea-ghost dwellings grow ferns and wild parsley, rosy pincushions of thrift and the ever-swinging flowers of the sea-campion which are like snow on the grass. The cracks of the rocks are filled with long straight lines of stonecrop, beaded like red coral, with tiny pink flowers. The effect is that of a paint brush which has been drawn over the rocks in straight red lines to mark every fault, every slip and division of surface. Far, far below the precipitous cliffs drop down to the sea, and above is the immense vault of a cloudless sky. It is a world beyond our planet, this Cornish coast.

Seagulls flash across from one pinnacle to another; on the cliff's edge the jackdaws flap their shining wings which here look like navy blue silk with grey satin. A fritillary butterfly hovers on a flower, and a hawk hovers over a slope a hundred feet below me, so that I can see the bright reddish-brown feathers of his back. Then, circling to gain height, he rises and flies across to the mainland. There is an unceasing murmur from the jade green sea as it beats on the rocks, and some of the low water rocks are covered with green slime the colour of young beech leaves in spring. Never a tree is in sight, and only the little twelfth century church stands dark as granite on the opposite hill across the water.

I stoop again to the stones, which are gemmed with money-wort, round crimson leaves like pence and green beaded flowers upright, perpendicular to the layers of rock. This Cornish plant is a decoration, for each circular leaf like a painted coin is pressed against the rock's face, each flower is a pyramid of pearly beads. The flowers stand so stiffly in the niches they look like the figures on Elizabethan tombs of rows of children kneeling with heads in descending ages. A fringe of foxgloves waves against the sky, with the bells clear on the blue background. The sullen roar of the sea comes booming now and then, from a cave where there is a blow-hole.

All day I have been here. In the afternoon I sat in a small 'meadow' of starry blue squills, the vernal squills, among the granite rocks of an overhanging cliff on the mainland. The crystalline quartz glitters like diamonds in the forest of grey lichen that nearly covers it. The lichens are prehistoric forests with hoary lilliputian trees about two inches high, whose outstretched boughs have no leaves or flowers. Here also the red-beaded stonecrops fill the crannies of the rocks, and tuffets of sea pinks, round and stiff, and the red pence of moneywort grows along the rock face, but the place is even more entrancing with the lavender blue flowers which star the grass at the foot of these outcrops of granite. Half a dozen stars rise on a blue-green stalk from the stiff threads of leaves. Nothing could be more beautiful than this miniature paradise of vernal squills growing in the lawn among the rocks, hanging at the edge of the cliff with the sea many feet below, so far away, the sounds are faint.

Seals live here in the inlet of the rocks, but I have not seen them this spring. A flock of oyster-catchers flies across to the upstanding rocks in the sea. Sometimes a gull comes to the rock near my head where I am hidden, and then it stares in astonishment as it sees me.

On June 2nd I went again to the island to sit in a monk's cell on the edge of a precipice which drops to the smooth green water. The cell is the size of an ordinary sitting-room, about twenty feet by twelve feet. The walls are built of irregular layers of stone, thin narrow layers in the two-feet-thick walls, with a cushion of soil smothered completely in flowers along the top. This surrounding wall is decked with moneywort along its face, like a hanging tapestry of rosy leaves and pyramidal flowers. On the top of the two-foot wall white sea-campion grows and sea pinks and a dwarf red sorrel, so thickly bound that all is flowered with a thick mat.

In the afternoon we drove up the long steep hills and over the Cornish moor to the village of Endillon, to see the church, for some months ago on a visit to Cornwall in autumn the hand-bell ringers from this church came to ring their bells and make music for us. Hand-bell ringing was a country pastime of our villages in Derbyshire, and people went a long way to hear the hand-bell ringers. So on this June 2nd morning we visited Endillon church. On the stone floor, bare as a dairy floor, were great yellow pancheons of wild flowers. They stood by the foot of the arches, sweet-scented and beautiful and simple.

In the church tower was a picture of six ringers in white shirts, red or black trousers, no hats, pulling six dancing bells above their heads. The inscription was as follows:

We ring the quick to Church, and dead to grave,
Good is our use, such usage let me have.
Who here therefore doth Damn, Curse or swear,
Or strike a quarrel though no Blood appear,
Who wears a Hatt, or Spurr, o'er turns a Bell,
Or by unskilful handling spoils a Peal
Shall sixpence pay for every single crime,
It will make him careful against another time.
Let's all in love and friendship hither come
Whilst the shrill treble calls to Thundring Tom
And since Bells are the model Recreation
Let's rise and Ring and fall to Admiration.

I returned from Cornwall with a collection of small trophies, pebbles striped and mottled, some with holes, which are lucky, some flat like pence, and some round like balls. Also I brought some King Arthur's trees from the cave where these miniature trees are found after high tide. They are swept up into Merlin's cave, and there they lie, but they are rare to find, and we walked in the cave at low tide seeking on the wet ledges of rock for them. They have magical properties, and they keep a house immune from danger of fire. So the Cornish people treasure them and there is always someone seeking for them to put on a mantelpiece, mounted on a small flat stand. They are remarkably like aged oaks, with boughs and trunk and twigs, sometimes in two dimensions, but the large trees, about 6 inches high which we only find in the wild storms of spring or winter, are in three dimensions. I use these brown trees as tiny tree backgrounds for a small crèche at Christmas, when they make a wood with the Holy Family sheltered among them.

Besides shells, stones and magical trees I have brought home some Cornish words for my collection, presented to me by a farm I visit. A 'bolley' is a stone picked up from the beach and used as a doorstep.

A 'critling' cake is a cake made of crisp roasted fat from a newly killed pig—the 'critlings' (which we called 'scratchings').

To 'shut in' a horse means to put the horse between the shafts of the cart and the same expression is used in Buckinghamshire.

And I brought a store of ghost tales—surely as nice a trunkful of fairings as anyone might find in a Cornish village.

FINANCIAL TRANSACTION

I have today, early in June, had the wind taken from my sails, the soft answer has been given which turneth away wrath, and I feel abashed, humbled and touched.

I was in the midst of an altercation with an important firm, a protest by letter against what I considered to be an iniquitous excess charge for some goods delivered. The official letters were business-like and unrelenting in their argument that my order had been fulfilled correctly. They thought they had a case, they had sent panels according to my measurement, and I felt, too, I had a case, they had not consulted me about a difficulty, and I had been grossly overcharged when a 'phone call would have put the matter right. I wrote a final letter, reiterating my arguments, and I asked, in a postscript, that my letter should go before the directors of the firm. There was little chance of anyone listening to my appeal in these days, but I made my protest.

By return the answer came. I left it till the end of my mail, unwilling to spoil the morning's beauty by reading a business letter with a curt refusal. At last I opened the letter. It was very short, with no signature, typed on the firm's notepaper with the Royal Appointment's crest at the top. I read to my astonishment, the following:

'Water Rat, Moldy Warp, Hare, Fuzzypeg and Squirrel present their compliments to Little Grey Rabbit and being aghast at the abominable depredations of the Weasels beg to enclose an amended account.'

With it was the account altered to even less than the amount I had claimed.

I replied as from one woodland animal to another.

'Grey Rabbit is very glad the wisdom of Wise Owl has prevailed and the pleas of Water Rat, Moldy Warp, Hare, Fuzzypeg and Squirrel have persuaded the Wicked Weasels to change their ways, and she has much pleasure in sending a cheque, on paper instead of on a beech leaf.'

The receipt came, 'With compliments,' and a delicious and clever pen and ink drawing of Wise Owl, with wide astonished eyes, sitting on a bough against the night sky, with the full moon behind him.

I think that only in England could such a transaction take place, and in these days it is a tonic and a gay sign that somebody's sense of humour remains.

OLD CUSTOMS

A Lincolnshire man wrote to me telling of old customs in his youth, remembering the small delights which stayed with him. On Saturdays he had a penny to spend, and he laid it out to great advantage in the village shop, after much cogitation and anticipation of the pleasures of riches.

A farthing was spent on Barber's Pole, which is the striped peppermint rock like the pink and white pole which projected from the booths of the barbers. And now I wonder where those poles have gone. Is there one left in the land?

A farthing's worth of Liquorice Ladders came next. This is perhaps the liquorice bootlaces which I saw in childhood. They

137

were loved by little boys, long and black and sticky ropes which lasted for hours.

A farthing's worth of Sherbet Suckers. I am not quite sure of these. Children bought sherbet, a powder, which was sold with a tiny tin spoon, in a woven Japanese box for twopence.

The last farthing went on A.B.C. biscuits. These were a childhood favourite, and they are still in the shops. Each small sweet biscuit was in the shape of a cut-out letter, and one could make words with them before they were eaten. X was a prolific letter, and many an OX was spelled and eaten. We never bought them in small quantities, they came by the pound from the grocer's, with the order, and a dish of them appeared on the tea-table, or we had a handful for a treat. We had no farthings, they were unknown, so we never had this fourfold division of a penny, and the cross little woman who kept the tiny ivy-covered sweetshop in the hamlet on the way to school would never have split a penny and provided four treats at a farthing each.

My correspondent went on to tell me that the country name for the cockchafer in Lincolnshire is Midsummer Dore. Snails are Oddmadods, as in Buckinghamshire.

A BUCKINGHAMSHIRE FARM

It is mid-June, and I have been to see my friends at the farm in the woods, whom I had no time to visit earlier in the month. We drove along the narrow winding lanes, whose banks were snowy with Queen Anne's Lace, where woods dipped down to the path, and mowing grass lay ready for the hay harvest. Five young weasels, very tiny, ran across the lane and disappeared in the hedge. Their tawny bodies and white undersides, their little waving tails made them look like some animals from heraldry as they moved in their sinuous motion across the way in front of the stationary car. We tried to see them in the field, but they had disappeared like smoke. Then a magpie flew over, and we bowed and wished him 'Good morning, sir,' to avert sorrow.

The farm lies in a hollow, below the road, a rose red collection of buildings like a small hamlet, with thatch and old brick and mossy tiled roofs, a dark red jewel set in the green of the woods. Woods surround the farm, they spread to the horizon on every side. No other house, no roof is in sight. Great chestnuts grow close to the farmhouse, casting a vast dense shade. I have never seen finer chestnuts than these giants, each symmetrical and perfect in shape.

The farmhouse is an old place, with rows of windows, and honeysuckle completely smothering the wall with a mass of crimson and yellow flowers, so densely packed it is a bower of honeybees and scent. Near the back door on the grass plat stands a thatched shed, used for wood-cutting and all the jobs of a farm. Its open front reveals the conglomeration of implement that bring back memories of other country folk—thatching pegs and wooden hayrakes, axes and hayforks, choppers and billhooks. A man was sharpening a scythe in the doorway, holding the blade on a log of wood, for the edge was broken. It was such a homely little place, so packed with memories of dogs and rabbits, of people sheltering from the rain, or escaping from the thraldom of daily tasks, of conversations with ancient labourers, of watching the craft of the woodman, the mender of hen coops and rabbit hutches, and chopping wood and perhaps a song and a whistle and a rough little dance that I could have lingered there for an hour.

The great barn took up one side of the farmyard. It was roofed with corrugated iron, for a fire had destroyed the thatch only a few years before. It was divided into several small outshuts, into one of which I peered to see the harness hanging on the wall. From the other outshuts came noises of horses, cows and pigs. At right angles to the great barn was a long low building of straw and wood. Its walls were rough pieces of timber interlaced with straw, and the roof was thatched, hanging low, so that one stooped to enter.

The roof was held up by tree trunks, pillars of wood, rough-hewn, beautiful and simple, primitive and strong. The front was open to air and light. It was the lambing hut, and a warmer and more comfortable place for ewes and their new-born lambs I do not know. The floor was covered with a thick litter of straw, soft as a carpet for small cloven feet.

In the farm kitchen is a large settle, curved round the fire-place, brought from an inn a hundred years ago. Everybody wishes to sit on this oak seat, which is draught-proof and warm, a place for talk and for eating and drinking. Its high back and cleverly contrived seating accommodation is the acme of modern comfort, and half a dozen can recline at ease, with pipes and tankards and country talk. Off the kitchen is the whitewashed dairy, and steps to a cellar, where once the casks of home-brewed ale were stored. The sitting-rooms are down the passage, where we stay a few minutes to see a dolls' house of huge size, furnished with the penny dolls and their household gear of fifty years ago. A good fire burned in the grate to ward away the chills of an English June, and round it were the horse brasses, many from the farm itself and a few sent by visitors.

The farmer is a bachelor, and his sister took us to see the well with its tradition of legend and escape. It is over 300 feet deep with water at the bottom, and it is never dry in the greatest drought. It was rather frightening in its atmosphere of peril and trouble of past days. Far below the surface there is an out-let, to a tunnel which leads to Chequers. A refugee could be let down by a rope to this entry, above the water surface, and then he could walk through the underground passage to safety. We saw the entrance to another tunnel which also leads to Chequers which is about three miles away. This tunnel has been partly explored in recent times, but the way was blocked with a fall of roof. Now the entrance has fallen, as a road was built over the tunnel and the weight of traffic has broken the chalk bank and destroyed all means of exploring this secret place.

Foxes abound here, and badgers live in perfect freedom, making sudden raids on the farm. The badgers tear the wood from the coops and get the chickens by sheer strength of claws. The foxes use wile and cunning and catch the straying hen and the careless pullet. At night one can hear the weird cry of the vixens, and the grunting call of the badgers in the woods. It is a farm where I feel much at home, a place within the woods, part of nature, with its cornfields opening to trees and bird life, and even a tractor looks different, as if it had its own natural life and stabling.

FLOWERS

I gathered a bunch of wild roses, some of the deepest pink, each petal veined with red, and the buds brilliant carmine. These bright pink roses grow on a bush near my house, and even the stalks and the twigs are rose-coloured, the thorns are small and the leaves tiny, and tinged with red. This is a special wild rose, such as we used to find on the limestone hills of childhood, and here it has chalk to feed it. I fear this marvel of a rose, which I look for each year, will be cut down and rooted away, for houses are to be built. Snow-white roses grow on another bush close to it, with long streamers of flowers, roses called the 'trailing dog-rose', packed with golden anthers, pure as white lilies. These are also called the Ayrshire roses. In Cornwall I picked the Burnet rose, from a rock hanging over the sea. I gathered the large creamy puff of the goat's beard, and some of its golden flowers with the long green sepals. We call it 'John-go-to-bed-at-noon', for it closes at midday. Agrimony and wild mignonette, salad burnet, dark brown and rosy red, grew in the lane verges. A field was purple with scabious flowers, a bedcover of mauve silk spread over the grass. In a wood grew white helleborines, and I added them to my bunch.

In a deserted chalk pit I found sainfoin, rosy pink tipped with red on each bean-shaped flower. There was wild mignonette, with yellowish green flowers, Greater Knapweed, and some yellow rock roses, all of them flowers of the chalk.

JUNE

I am in Penn Church with its whitewashed walls, and the painted Doom, showing the Last Judgement. Little boys in maroon blazers and grey trousers fill the first two pews, and one turns and smiles at me, for he is my friend. We sing ancient hymns, we praise God, we listen to the terrible story of Sisera, and again I feel the pain in my temple as Jael hammers the long nail through the Captain's head as he sleeps in her tent. It is a story that has brought horror to my heart from childhood days when I heard it in our little church by the side of the river, when I saw in imagination the soldier lying on the lawn, nailed to the grass. Did the same indignation and anger fill the hearts of the rows of little boys as they listened? I wondered. Or were they used to horrors of war and bombs and cruelties, such as we had never imagined?

We sang 'Holy, Holy, Holy, Lord God Almighty', we prayed for peace and we thanked God for all the blessings of life. The stout old retired clergyman mounted the pulpit and preached his excellent sermon on the modern theory of the Universe, the original discoveries of Copernicus and Galileo, the pushing back of space, the changing ideas of God as the Universe expanded through knowledge, and all the little boys stared and listened. So we were swept into the stars, as we sat in the small church, beneath that ancient oak roof with its Queen posts and hammer beams.

GOOD-BYE CUCKOO

On this cool June day, I saw my first bee-orchis this year. A young girl had found them and now they were given to me. We have a pact for wild flowers. I sent some white helleborines to this country girl and she found the bee-orchis in the field near her cottage for me.

Dog-daisies and patches of yellow birds' foot grew by the road, and on the cricket ground the sight screens were ready for the Sunday cricket match. I drove round the valley through a quiet lovely lane between beech woods. Dog-roses filled the hedges and I stopped to pick them in a triangle of grass by a large farm. There magnificent beech trees grow, and some firs, striking and fine specimens, which look strange and foreign in this place.

Over the hedge the cattle grazed, a herd of thirty, Herefords and a few Jerseys, and by the gate which led to this field the dog-roses sprayed their flowers, to brush the coats of beasts passing through to the milking. The grass was long by the side of the road, for the gypsies seem to have deserted this part of the county. There was enough feeding for a herd of cattle on the verges, if anyone could be found to keep them safe.

June 24th. There was the cuckoo saying good-bye on its minor note and nobody took any notice. 'I'm going on a long journey. Good-bye,' it called, and I answered 'Good-bye. A safe journey.'

The same day I was turning the pages at random of a small volume of Shakespeare, and I saw these words, startling in their aptness, and quite unexpected.

> *He was but as the Cuckoo in June,*
> *Heard but not regarded.*

For the call was the last I heard, and the cuckoo flew away, on this Midsummer Day. It was a sad little call, I thought, this farewell, or perhaps I projected my own feelings into it, saying good-bye.

Broadcasts, books, articles all attack the cuckoo, as if it could change its habits, conquer its ancient way of living. As soon expect the bird to warble like a blackbird as to conform to our idea of respectability and polite manners regarding private property in nests.

YOUNG BIRDS

In these last days of June there is great excitement in the

garden, with mothers feeding the insistent little birds, who run about flapping their wings and crying. It is an amusing sight to see these little creatures, who are so tame one can get very near. Under the kitchen window in the japonica bush the thrush had her nest, and there she sat, taking no notice of passers-by, of opening windows and talking people. She was so still that once I thought she must be dead, but when I put my face close to hers, screened in the thick leaves I saw her sparkling eye. Thrushes sit with beaks upraised as if they were listening to every sound. Then the little fat thrushes were hatched and a twittering cry came to the watchers. At last they were able to leave the nest, to explore, to struggle for their first flight to the low railing, where the mother fed them. Now they are hopping all over the lawn with another family of babies, and young blackbirds, and sparrows. The robins in another bush hatched out some time ago, and this year the flycatcher has left my garden, to my sorrow, for the row of little flycatchers sitting on the aerial of the wireless set was a charming sight.

Blackcap and willow wren sing every morning with rapture, and the blackbirds sing as if they were singing at the dawn of the world. Never have they sung so sweetly or so long. They have been tamer than usual, perhaps because no neighbours have cats, and they are unafraid.

My Scottie lies and watches them feed from his food dish a foot away. He is interested in them, and will not come indoors until they have finished their feast. Sometimes he looks round at me, with an expression that resembles a smile, as he shares my own pleasure. He keeps still, as if unwilling to disturb them, and the robins hop almost to his black nose end. Yet he is fierce as a tiger when a postman comes to the house, he springs on the man's boot, and although there are several postmen in this district, he is the enemy of the whole tribe. He refuses to be cajoled by kind words, he attacks without warning, and it is not a defence of the house for he growls and barks in the car when he sees one of these enemies innocently going on his daily round.

JUNE

A writer to the daily paper suggested that the reason a dog hates postmen is because he never sees his master or mistress invite the postman indoors for a cup of tea. In my youth we always invited the postman into the kitchen to have a cup of hot tea with a good lashing of cream and sugar, and he drank it on the hearthstone in front of the fire, as he gave his news of the world. He was our link with the goings-on of civilisation, he brought election results, and deaths and births and removals and sales. One of the most dramatic events he brought to us which I remember was the news of Queen Victoria's death. He must have had an extra cup of tea and piece of hot toast that morning of snow, as we listened aghast at the sad news. But *always* the dogs barked furiously and struggled to destroy him.

Sussex Journey

From June 26th to June 29th we explored Sussex, thinking of it as a foreign country, for neither my friend nor I knew much about it. We had hardly crossed the borders except by train, but we knew it was a country of beauty and renown. Yet it was not so much a visit to a strange land as a voyage through time, and we were breathless and lost in the speed of motion through the years. We were in the time of the Norman Conquest at Battle Abbey, with the site of the battle only a mile or two away and the mighty walls of the Abbey so strong and enduring around us. Even as we drove near we met a motor cyclist with a helmet on his head, like a Norman, speeding furiously towards us, along the road which had the signpost BATTLE. HASTINGS. He might have been carrying the news of victory, and we, poor English, were defeated. I think that signpost was as startling as the one I first saw in Buckinghamshire, pointing to the ICKNIELD WAY.

We were in the early nineteenth century at the Cross-in-Hand windmill, with its sails turning slowly, clacking gently, talking to the wind, while a lorry instead of a great cart stood near laden with sacks of maize, which it took through the gate.

JUNE

We were in an eldritch company when a great number of bats flew over our heads from a grove of sycamore trees at Lewes where we stayed the first night. We stood there in the twilight and the bats circled us and darted near, so that I wanted to sing our old song as I tried to lure them.

> *Bat, bat, come under my hat,*
> *And you shall have a piece of bacon.*

We were in a mixture of Elizabethan days and Victorian at Batemans where we entered Rudyard Kipling's house. The great red brick house, beautiful to see, is Elizabethan, but there was a heavy Victorian atmosphere within, and I felt that I was an unwelcome intruder to Kipling's privacy. So I went out to the gardens and lawns, the ponds and the trees. Even there the depression followed me, darkened by the statuettes, but a mighty willow grew on the grass, so old that it could have been a contemporary of the house. It was the willow in which Puck might have hidden, and the willow saved Batemans for me.

At Ditchling we went over the sixteenth century house called Wing Place, a house where Anne of Cleves is said to have lived. It was bought for her by Henry VIII after the divorce, and a warm comfortable house it seemed to be. The doors had iron latchets and hinges of leather. The garden, sloping down with grass path and many flowering trees, and Ditchling Beacon beyond, was a perfect secret garden. The sun filtered through and we were happy.

We stayed for the second night at Rye, in the fifteenth century Mermaid Inn, with hidden staircases and rooms and doorways, and tales of smugglers, and ghosts and hauntings. We went into the house of Henry James, and I paid secret homage to the memory of the man who wrote many books I loved long ago.

We went to Fittleworth, and stood on the little bridge to sketch the Mill House, with its fairytale round arches over the mill stream, and its hipped red roof and dormers. It was seventeenth century, and Rex Whistler might have drawn it for

Hans Andersen. Water crowfoot flowered on the backwaters, and moorhens and coots waded there.

We climbed to the top of Ditchling Beacon to see the view along with several people in cars. We saw Mouse Lane at Little Beeding, and Arundel Castle and Pevensey Castle and Bodiam. We drove in the moonlight past the foot of Chanctonbury Ring, but it was too late to climb there; we passed a lane which led to a Roman villa; and we saw the tents of a county cricket match. Like the three jovial huntsmen, we had to leave these things behind, as we hunted and we hollooed along the way to Chichester for the third night. We saw the Cathedral with its early carvings of the Raising of Lazarus, and Martha and Mary, and the Bell Tower and the Butter Cross.

At Rye at the Mermaid Inn, on the night of June 27th, I dreamed of a man with bloodstained head, hanging back, near the ground, his face visible, very white and his eyes closed, and he was near to me so that I saw him very clearly, with the blood on his head and hair. There was no legend or story of any tragedy, but the man was very real to me, and I thought perhaps he once lived there and was slain.

On the 29th as we drove towards home through Surrey, we were held up for a minute by a group of workmen in the road, and we swerved slowly past. I looked down to find the obstruction. A man with bloodstained head, hanging back, his white face visible, his hair in fair thick locks, his eyes closed, was held in the arms of one of the men, close to the ground, and we passed a yard away. It was the man about whom I had dreamed; he had just been knocked down by a van which stood near. Shocked and shivering we went on and the ambulance was driven up. It was the merest chance we arrived at that particular moment, out of the whole of time, the few minutes when he was held with his head in that poise of unconsciousness or death.

So time future, as well as time past was included in that visit to Sussex, in June, and somehow it seemed an important journey, with experience of time past and time to come, and we really had travelled beyond the present.

JULY

BUMBLE BEE

I sit in the garden early in July, on a cool day, the wind sweeping the beech trees with the sound of rushing water as tree tops sway caught by this rough north blast. It is a presage of rain, this movement of the leaves, turning their silvery undersides, this noise of complaining trees, but there is no sign among the flowers and bees, for we are completely sheltered by the belt of woodland.

Lemon-yellow snapdragons grow in front of the roses in a border close to my chair. A jay flies over shrieking angrily, and young blackbirds sun themselves with open wings spread out on the warm soil under some of the rose trees. I am a stick, a stone, they do not see me. The Madonna lilies are in bloom, very near to me, twenty tall white lilies with several flowers on each still stem, pure and ineffably sweet, and there are Excelsior foxgloves, yellow and fawn and cream, survivors of a vast company which I grew from seed, but they swamped my small garden and had to be uprooted. This is one of my seasons for flowers, and then will come a long gap with only a flower here and there.

There is a continual rustle and flutter around me—birds feeding their young, babies trying to fly, babies squeaking and talking, in a bird-world we forget exists. The raspberries are ripe, and blackbirds dive over the hedge into the canes, swooping like little black aeroplanes, and then they rise again, squawking, startled, as they see me sitting silently near with my book and pen. I am a scarecrow, a spoil-sport, sitting in their garden, with a robin near of course, looking at me, hopping to my feet.

I have been watching a bumble-bee, which goes from flower to flower of the snapdragons, backing out after completely disappearing inside. This rear action always gives me great satisfaction. It reminds me of a shaggy carthorse, backing out of the stable door to the sunshine. The furry legs of the bee resemble the shaggy legs and feathered feet of a Shire horse.

I try an experiment. I close a snapdragon, and hold it quietly between finger and thumb with the bee inside. There is silence, no buzz of anxiety, no protest, all is still, and I wait half a minute, which must be like an hour, with the closed door of yellow petals concealing the bumble-bee. What are the feelings of the bee shut up in the cave of gold? I take away my fingers, and the bee comes out, face foremost, and, I thought, much surprised. How had it turned round within the flower? I had seen no movement. It sat on the lip of the snapdragon, and busily cleaned off the yellow pollen which dusted its body and legs during the enforced imprisonment. Then it flew to the next flower as if nothing had happened. Evidently I was a natural phenomenon, a wind that had closed the flower up.

So, when the bee disappeared in the orifice, I closed the snapdragon again and imprisoned the little creature. Again there was no sound, no buzz of anger, a patience and a waiting. I opened my fingers, and the bee saw me as it came out. There was no doubt about it. I, and not nature, was the source of its imprisonment. Away flew the bee, far away, right over the flowers, far into the air, away from inquisitive human beings.

ROSES

Behind these snapdragons Mme Pierre Oger, the exquisite one, the beauty, holds up her pale pink flowers. These are quite enchanting, and I feel I am watching something in a fairytale as I contemplate them. The small round cups are like the china in a doll's tea-service, or like the shell roses under the glass case in a Victorian parlour. Each petal is deeply curved, each flower is spherical, some are shaded pink and white, some rosy; others white, and they change colour with the weather. In August they will be different and again in September they will alter. On certain days they are so pale and wan with the hot sun I feel pale and wan in sympathy. They are too sad to be gathered. On other days they are radiantly happy, bright pink, eager to look around, and again they must not be picked because they are too beautiful. They seem to lose something of their perfection when they are gathered. I have had this Bourbon rose only a year, and I always visit it first thing in the morning, to find a new surprise, either in the colour or in the opening round cups. Mme Pierre Oger is dated 1879, but the Bourbons are a cross between the old Damask roses and the China roses dating from the eighteenth century.

Next to Mme Pierre Oger is the Queen of Denmark, a full-petalled rose, of the most ravishing pink, with a centre like a much-wrapped and crinkled package. The leaves are bluish-green, and this combination of colour, the perfection of the pink against the glaucous green makes this a royal rose, and a famous one. The Albas have been grown in England since the Middle Ages, and this old-fashioned rose is quite one of the most beautiful. It occurs in an Ambrose Brueghel, a flower piece of roses and lilies in an open basket, painted in 1640 to 1650, together with a white rose which might be a Madame Hardy rose.

JULY

I have another Rosa Alba, called Celestial, which grows freely in a border by the wood. It is about seven feet high with long streamers and semi-double roses like wild ones, whose long narrow buds are so perfect, they seem beyond compare. The roses are shell-pink, lighter than the Queen of Denmark roses, and the leaves are blue-green.

Many roses of the Rosa Mundi are out; they started in June and they have not finished. They are flowers of enchantment that ravish the senses of susceptible people like me. I go very early in the morning to find the new roses, for they bloom in the night, and I see the newly opened flowers with their carmine stripes already jewelled with dew drops. I fill a glass container, an old wine glass, which shows the stalks and leaves and flowers to perfection, for nothing must be missed in this visual feast. The alternate and irregular red and pink stripes on the curved petals are the feature of this Gallica rose. The name is associated with the Fair Rosamund, mistress of Henry II, but this legend is now supposed to be incorrect. Once I believed that she was hidden in a thicket of these rose trees, in that famous maze, which only those who knew the secret could penetrate. The Rosa Mundi was well-known in 1640, but I have seen no paintings of it among the Dutch and Flemish artists of that period except in a picture by Van Verendael, (d. 1691). Shakespeare may refer to it in Sonnet 130; 'I have seen roses damask'd, red and white.'

This is not the York and Lancaster Rose, also striped red and white. Rosa Mundi is far more beautiful, the red is carmine, and the stripes distinct and clear. The painter Ehret made a fine painting of Rosa Mundi, in the eighteenth century.

There is a modern striped rose across the garden, called 'Modern Times', a new version of the Rosa Mundi, rather coarse and florid in its colouring. It is like a piece of crudely-painted pottery compared to a cup of Rockingham china.

William Lobb was my first old-fashioned moss-rose, and I waited impatiently to see its flowers. The buds are crimson and mossy, and the rose is flat, small, purple-red and quite enchant-

151

ing, with its little petals tightly packed together in a plate of perfume. It hangs over, and sends out many little branches and many roses, untidy and delightful, careless of stakes, smothered with flowers.

There are pink moss-roses and red ones, but the best is Blanche Moreau, a white moss with heavily mossed flowers. I pick bunches of these rose buds for small gifts, before the flowers are fully out, to be left on doorsteps, for they are like Victorian valentines or birthday cards. The two bushes grow well, they droop over with the weight of the flowers, but they are prone to greenfly later on in the summer.

A very early rose is Canary Bird. I saw this first at the Chelsea Show and ordered one. It grows very fast and sends out long sprays with the tiny yellow roses perched on them like the canaries of its name.

Another favourite, perhaps the one I would choose if I might have only one rose in the world, is the Mermaid so well-known and loved. It has single roses of great beauty and delicacy of texture, which grow in clusters. The bud is sharply-beaked, the large rose opens wide to disclose a bunch of gold stamens.

The foliage stays on the tree during winter, and long new red shoots spring up, with secondary sprays at right angles so that it is difficult to make the rose follow any special direction. It is a most determined rose, which knows what it wants and springs out to catch the postman's cap, or to sweep the veil from my Sunday hat.

Near Celestial, on the windy side of the garden there grows a rose I adore. I have known it all my life. We called it in childhood the Damask rose, but it is the Red Gallica. It resembles the Rosa Mundi, in shape and form and growth, but it is unstriped. The shape of the loose petals is fascinating. Several bushes of this "Damask rose" grew in our kitchen garden, with an old wall as a background, facing due south, and in that warm sheltered place it flourished. It had been there in my great-grandfather's time, I was told, before our house was rebuilt. I carried bunches to school for the teacher, and picked flowers for the table. Their life was short, but the roses followed one another with rapidity during June. Their semi-double flowers, with thick gold stamens where bees always feasted, were examined and admired by my infant eyes, as I strayed in that garden, lost from human beings, escaped from the busy grown-up world, to find myself in a land of fantasy. There grew these glowing old red roses, which I was allowed to pick because they were not important being so old-fashioned, and bushes of thyme, where a toad might lurk, and parsley beds where a baby might lie in hiding, and small trees of sage and the herb garden. The Gallica is one of the oldest roses known, and it was brought from the East by the Crusaders in the days of the Saracens. It was grown by the Persians in 1200 B.C. So with immunity and child joy I picked the petals and tried to make the Elixir of Roses, which I had heard of in some book, perhaps the banned *Arabian Nights Entertainment*.

Another rose of my early years which I still try to discover was a white many-petalled flat rose, with green centre, and it grew in great abundance upon one special bush, about six feet tall, with literally hundreds of flowers at once. It too was in the kitchen garden, but we picked bunches from it to carry wherever we went, in market basket, in hot hands, by pony trap or by train. It had no greenfly, no disease, it grew like an angel, spreading sweet perfume around it. Yet I have never seen this rose at Chelsea or in any garden or show. It resembled Madame Hardy, but was not quite the same. It was one of the Albas, an old Cheshire and Derbyshire rose.

Cardinal de Richelieu is a beautiful rose, with its dark purple flower and its velvet petals. I have two or three bushes, small, for it never grows very high. It is a Rosa Gallica, one of the early roses of the world.

A DRIVE

July 7th was a marvel of a day, with sunshine and sweet airs and beauty. Friends took me to Marlow, and we crossed the suspension bridge, driving slowly to see the swans and the boats and the glittering flashing water of the Thames below. I always feel excited on a bridge, and Marlow bridge with its long span and the tranquil scene of the swans below is a delight. We went along a road through the woods to Temple, and in the narrow road as we dipped down the hill we met a tractor with wreaths of flowering honeysuckle bound round the bonnet of the machine and on the caps of the red-cheeked young men. There was a great load of baled hay, and the whole enormous mechanical vehicle stopped in a gateway of the fields for us to pass. If we had met it in the lane, with its hay touching both sides, we should have had to reverse a long way uphill to escape. Wild roses grew in the hedges, deep pink ones, so that we cried out, 'Look! Look!' as we passed.

We went to Wargrave, and up Crazy Hill to Henley to see the splendid bridge, then back through Hambleden and Medmenham to Marlow to have tea at the 'Compleat Angler', on the lawn close to the river. We wandered to the weir which flows down a long flight of curved steps, and on a step in the rushing water stood a heron, quietly fishing, with no concern for us who watched it so near.

'It's a lucky omen to see a heron fishing,' I was told, and indeed it is a lucky sight to see, for herons are special birds. Perhaps they fished here when the Romans came up the Thames and the Danes harried the valleys.

We crossed the bridge again and stayed by the lock to see the boats pass through the gates, and the water seep into the lock while young boys helped the lock-keeper. There was a little cart laden with hay going along the narrow road, a contrast to the great tractor and lorry full of baled hay we had seen earlier.

MEDMENHAM AND HAMBLEDEN

The Thames is a homely happy river as it flows through the south of Buckinghamshire, between green low meadows and beech woods. It is not too wide, not too swift, it looks clean and very beautiful with yellow water-lilies in its shallows and meadowsweet in cream foam on its banks. The swift water which tumbles over the weirs at Hambleden seems unlike the placid stretch of the water at Medmenham or the clear river at Marlow and Little Marlow.

The willow-haunted ferry at Medmenham, where a boat takes a passenger across the river to the Berkshire bank, is down a narrow lane with a few old houses by the sides and blue geranium and meadowsweet in the ditch. Medmenham was once famed for its notorious Abbey, a seat of the Hellfire Club who called themselves the Medmenham Monks, but now the house, shielded by its curtains of weeping willows, is shriven and at peace in its lawns by the Thames close to the ferry.

The old ferryman spent his time in a wooden hut whose roof is covered with wooden shingles, and I often sat with him there talking about his carpentry days and the boat building and the busy ferry which was used in earlier times to avoid the journey to Marlow. I cheered his lonely time, for he had few visitors, and the ferry was not often wanted. He was a fine craftsman, and his tools which were ranged neatly round the sides of the long shed and workroom were mostly inherited from his father, also a boatbuilder. Their handles were worn by use, the blades thin and shining, and he had initials carved and little signs of his own cut in the wood. Now he is dead, and I miss his companionship when I go to see the river.

Flood marks of the Thames are marked on the hut, and a post with high tide records stands in the water. The river sometimes sweeps up over the banks and reaches a high level on the ferry hut.

The Thames was crossed at this ferry by Charles II in 1678 and again by Queen Victoria and by George V. These royal crossings are recorded on a dark weatherworn piece of wood above the door of the ferryman's hut.

A few yards beyond the ferry, on the towpath, a monument stands, with a triumphant cherub waving his hand on the summit. It is one of those quite English monuments commemorating somebody's fight for freedom against an oppressor, and here it is the right to have a ferry. Buckinghamshire is a home for these lost causes. John Hampden's cross near Prestwood was erected overlooking the land that was sold to pay his fine when he opposed Charles I for Ship Money.

Jordan's Hostel records the struggles of Quakers against oppression.

The banks of the Thames at Medmenham are bordered with reeds and flowers, with purple loose-strife in long spikes, with meadow-sweet, and blue wild geranium, with the lovely white comfrey which always makes me think of witches' brews and herbalists, for I heard many a tale of its powers in my childhood. Its white bells always fascinate me. Then there are the tawny gold flowers of American balsam, the Touch-me-not, which fade away before one can get them home. They are the most fragile of flowers, although they look sturdy, but they die like fish without water.

The water-mill at Hambleden was our next stopping place, and there we rejoice at the business which still goes on in a country where so many old mills are derelict. This mill has an ancient tradition, it was mentioned in the Domesday book, and it is the proud boast that it has been working ever since.

As one goes through the gates into the mill yard there is a hum and rumble of wheels, a mist of fine grist and an air of busy work. A dusty white man peeps out of a cobwebbed white window, belts move through the floors, and my friend the miller sits in his office with several cats coming and going.

The miller's house stands near, with a little lawn and a great cedar, which bears lavender cones on its flat boughs. Behind the house is a row of cottages, once occupied by the workmen and now falling to pieces, but still beautiful with their timbers and ancient brickwork and roofs. A tree has seeded itself in the wall of one of the cottages, and it springs out from the side of an upper window. House-leek and ferns grow in the crumbling old red brick walls.

The mill itself is white as snow, glittering with new paint on its weather-boarded sides, and its reflection in the Thames is a constant allure for artists. Tall reeds and brown grasses grow in this backwater, feathery grasses which form part of the scene. On top of the mill is a small square cupola with ironwork weather-vane and once I had the felicity of climbing up the long ladders in the mill and standing in the high room under this lantern.

Hambleden Mill has turbines and rollers, but for centuries it was worked only by water power. The mill wheel has gone, steel rollers have come and the flour and grist are carried away by lorries instead of by boats. Now the water is in full spate dashing down the deep fall of the sluice, and the wind is strong enough to keep us from walking across the long wooden foot-bridges which span the Thames, and lead to the lock gates on the Berkshire side. The water is churned white as it dashes against the sides of the lock, but the centre is deep green, smooth and swift and very powerful. There is an element of magic and fairytale, of ancient wisdom and eternity in this place. It is a spot to which I often return, in winter and in summer, for always there is a diversity in the colour of the water, in the shapes of waves and crests of foam which fall down under the slight structure of the foot-bridges.

YOUNG JAY

Yesterday, July 10th, a young jay came down to my garden, and sat about three yards away from my chair, among the daisies of the lawn. It could not fly, and it rested close to me, unafraid. After a time it must have realised there was water near, so it managed to scramble into the shallow bird bath, and there it squatted and drank. I had a good view for it stayed at least two hours. I left it still crouching near my chair, eating nothing.

The breast is covered with exquisite warm-coloured brown down, like a sealskin coat, its tail is black, only a stump, and its black wings have a white patch on each. The lovely blue feathers against its sides have pale fawn tips, and these are the little feathers country workmen used to put in their hat bands. The head seems to be striped today, the 11th, but yesterday it was brown and silky. Its eyes are blue, a marvellous colour.

Now it eats a crust, for I feared it would starve. It holds it with a toe and works away at it. It struggles with the bread, bending it this way and that, pressing it on the grass, and a chaffinch hopping near looks alarmed. All the birds keep away while the baby jay is in the garden. It is extremely tame, and I could easily hold it. Then, after I have left it as dusk settles, it goes to a patch of mint and sleeps there for the night. It stayed with me for three days and then managed to fly to a low bough.

YOUNG WOODPECKER

Today, July 14th, I noticed a young green woodpecker in my garden, its feathers awry as if some of them had been broken, and I feared it had perhaps been hurt. It stayed very still, only stretching tiny wings now and then and waiting. I waited too. There is a strange deep feeling of calm in waiting for something to happen. No telephone can be answered, nobody can be seen. One is invisible. I hoped the parents would come back for I had seen them fly away, disturbed. I felt rather anxious about this small bird, but I resisted an impulse to go to it, perhaps frighten it.

After about twenty minutes stillness on both our parts, the little woodpecker flapped its short wings and moved a short distance. It gazed round at me. I could see the immature beak and the round inquiring eye. I was nobody, nothing, very still by the open french window. It sat hunched on the grass, a little green and yellow ball. Then it flapped its wings and waddled a short distance to a small apple tree. It gazed intently at this tree, and to my surprise it began to climb a few inches, to pick the ants and flies sticking to the band round the trunk. After a time it fell down, but it pecked at the ground unconcernedly. Then it waddled to a small plum tree and climbed the slender trunk a few inches, and pecked at the bark. I think it was the first time it had ever climbed, for down it tumbled, and there it stayed,

more confident in its powers and serene. It moved over the grass
and flapped its small wings with better flapping and ease. Soon
its parents came down to join it, and I realised they must have
been watching it from the wood. They flew away, the small
green woodpecker rising up with them.

WRYNECKS

This afternoon, July 17th, I put some cheese rinds on the
two bird tables, and about an hour later I heard strange sounds
of unknown birds. A flock of wrynecks had come, and as I have
never seen these birds except singly or a pair I was delighted.
The cheese had brought them, but how such shy visitors discovered it, I do not know. I had plenty of time to watch them
for they walked near my windows, and displayed their feathers
and twisted their necks, and behaved like a company of
strangers who had come to see a sight. With them a gold-
finch, but this charmer soon flew away, after swinging on a tall
mullein stalk. The wrynecks talked and made little noises, they
bathed in the bird bath and explored the garden. There must
have been twenty on a summer excursion, a trip to investigate.

An old Buckinghamshire countryman used to talk to me
about the wryneck which was much more common in his youth.
He called it the 'Cuckoo's Mate', and he knew no other name,
so at first I could not discover what he meant. It comes a few
days before the cuckoo—'to prepare the way', he said. It leaves
in late August or early September.

Other local country names are Cuckoo's Maiden and
Cuckoo's Messenger, Snake-bird, Tongue-bird, Emmet-
hunter, Long-tongue and Barley Bird. Kilvert speaks of 'a bird
as big as a thrush, brown with a black head, which comes along
with the cuckoo and is called the "Cuckoo's Fool".'

On July 23rd I saw a young cuckoo fly across from a neigh-
bouring garden and settle in a chestnut tree, but of course there
was never a call. Two little wrens fluttered in my garden, perching on a tree stump, and carrying on a conversation. They often

visit me, but they are so shy, so quick, so demure, they keep so low and so invisible, I often see only the little stumpy tail disappearing. They like the rock garden, where the small plants suit their small stature.

The Regale lilies and the Madonna lilies are out in great beauty, tall and beautiful with many deep bells. I shall plant more lilies.

As I sat writing in my garden two delights occurred. A dishevelled peacock butterfly perched on my finger and stayed there, poised on my forefinger which grasped my pen. I think it was perhaps a ragged butterfly I once fed with sugar in early spring, if such a recognition were possible. Then a blue dragonfly flew over the bird bath and I could hear the beating of its wings. I was delighted to hear this delicate sound, for no longer can I hear the high squeak of the bats, as once I heard them every night. Now their vibration is beyond my ears, which are attuned to lower sounds.

RAIN

The angle of the falling rain changes as one looks, it swings from a slope of perhaps 60 degrees with the earth to perpendicular, and with it the sound varies from a deep note to a soft musical shirr. Even as I write the rain has turned through the right angle and now it falls from the west. The trees lift their branches up and down, gently falling with rain and rising to their normal position, a lovely motion like myriad waving hands of green. The boughs of the hornbeam, between the great beech and the tall oak tree, move more violently. This has always been so, and there is a shiver in those light leaves when the beech tree is comparatively still. The hornbeam seems to press forward, to make itself felt and seen, for it is pushed in the background by two giants, beech and oak. Like a fern it holds out its fronds, and the gap below shelters foxgloves and a flight of low steps from the scrap of woodland to the lawn.

The surface of the shallow stone trough for birds is dimpled with rain, as spirals appear to rise and circles revolve. A row of raindrops hang from a little low table, evenly spaced, like silver bells. They drop at irregular intervals, some of them quickly, and others waiting here for a long time before they fall. In childhood these raindrops pendant from roofs of outbuildings or hanging from the flat tops of the stone walls, were a constant source of pleasure as we sat in the stable or barn and watched them and gave them names, and pitted one against another. So prisoners may enjoy themselves, but we were free to go out and join in the fun by watching the spring water pour into the troughs, or by gazing at the downpour from the roof to the water-tubs.

The leaves of the lilies are beaded with silver globules, like the flowers that were there in May. These smooth green pointed leaves are upright, with tips lifted like the drinking woodpeckers which have now invaded the lawn. Three young green wood-peckers have flown silently down by my window. They have begun to dig under an apple tree. They drive in their sharp beaks, they shake their crimson caps, they glance around at me every few seconds.

My movement has startled them, silently they fly away with a yellow sheen of wings to the wood, one after another. I can hear their cries now as they rest in the trees. I wish I had gone from the window and left them in peace.

The lead boy rides his dolphin in the rain, as if he were breasting the sea splashed by the waves. The bright colour of wet lead shines in his arms and on the leg that encircles the dolphin's body. A lead statue comes alive in the rain; it glows with silver light, and the curves of the great dolphin, the heavy head with round eyes, the scaled body, the forked tail, all gleam with vitality and secret living. This seems to be an attribute of lead, this metal I adore, for although there is the saying 'as heavy as lead' or leaden-eyed, it is a bright living metal when it is not asleep. It is warm as a living creature, it is ancient and kind.

L

POTPOURRI

I have been making potpourri with the rose petals from the scented roses in my garden for the first time. I picked the full-blown roses each morning, chiefly red and white roses and old-fashioned roses. I sprinkled the petals on cardboard trays in the porch to dry in the sun, but not in direct sunshine, adding more petals every day until I had several tray loads. Wind and rain had to be circumvented, and the trays were rushed indoors when a shower fell.

When the leaves were dry I added common salt, which again had to be dried out. I put many fragrant herbs among the roses —scented geranium leaves, thyme, bay and lemon balm, clove carnations, rosemary and lavender. The rose petals were put in layers in a deep bowl, a large blue container, and pressed down with a spicy mixture sprinkled on each layer. The mixture was made from as many as possible of the following ingredients:

> 1 *ounce of Gum Benzoin*
> 1 *ounce each of:*
> *Angelica root*
> *and Cloves.*
> *A pinch of Nutmeg grated,*
> *and Cinnamon.*
> 4 *ounces of Orris root.*
> 2 *ounces of oil of Bergamot, but I also added*
> *Bergamot leaves and flower petals.*
> ½ *ounce of oil of Geranium, if no geranium leaves.*
> *Slices of thin lemon rind.*
> ½ *ounce of oil of Lavender.*

I shall stir the contents of the bowl every day, for a month, and keep covered between the stirrings. Then I shall turn out the potpourri into china bowls.

JULY

GLOW-WORMS

My daily paper has this supercilious note on glow-worms, which are shining in the hedges now. ' "Among the crooked lanes, in every lane, the Glow-worm lights his gem and through the dark a moving radiance twinkles." These words were written 150 years ago. Today we would scorn to speak in such terms of the luminescence emitted by a species of Lampyridae.'

The glow-worms have deserted my lane since houses have been built, but not long ago there were many little green lights shining among the leaves when I went out at dusk. Sometimes I carried a few home with me on their leaves, and set them among the pinks and pansies. The light from each one was astonishing. I have read small print by the light of a glow-worm, whose beams illuminated leaves and flowers around it.

A glow-worm would shine for three nights in my garden and then disappear, when it had presumably found a mate. Once I had twenty-six little green lights in the borders and grass, and another time I saw about thirty glowing in the road, spaced at intervals as if they had been placed to light up the night. I could see the green light from a glow-worm at a distance of about eighty feet down my garden. A year ago I saw one little creature in the garden here and now none are left. They appear in hedge bottoms and on banks and field verges, not, as far as I know, in the middle of fields, and we found them in childhood by the milking paths, and in the garden, on the steep banks of the lanes, where their light shone out, and on the edges of the lawn.

TIGRIDIAS

Last February, feeling rather feeble after bronchitis, I crept out of doors to the sunshine. Pulchella Violet Queen was flowering bravely and a few snowdrops. With a trowel I dug a shallow grave in the edge of the rock garden and hurriedly planted some tiny bulbs which had arrived that morning. I had bought them by chance. Then back I went to bed. The winds blew, the snow covered the ground, and winter returned with full force and severity.

One March day I found the directions for planting these small brown bulbs, whose exotic name is Tigridias. They were not hardy! They should not be planted until all fear of frost had gone, and May was the best month. I went out at once with peat to cover them and cloches to drape over them, but I feared I was too late, for my pipes had burst and frost was everywhere. I smothered them in the brown peat blanket, and hoped that the ice had not completely slain them. They grew, they thrust through the peat, and held up fine grass spikes, but I kept them within the cloches until they were too tall for the low tents. Then I forgot all about them. They grew taller and thicker, but nothing happened. Other flowers bloomed, the rock garden was gay with miniature tulips and pinks and alpine flowers, and this grassy edge stayed the same.

One day in late July, I was starting off for a visit to get a breath of sea air before the crowds invaded the coast. Just as I shut the front door and took a glance round to see that all was safe I saw the vision. The Tigridias had burgeoned in the night. On the path's edge were wonderful flowers with three large petals apiece, tawny and orange, crimson and shrimp pink, golden and fawn, yellow and lemonish, each flower different and unique.

I nearly stayed at home. I was astonished as though a flight of Arabian Nights' Princesses had alighted in the garden. Their robes were as lovely as silks from Persia and India. Their shape was delicate, three large petals and within three differently coloured sepals or petals, spotted and prinked and tiger-marked. I had never expected flowers like these from the insignificant pictures on the bulb list. I had not been prepared for so much beauty.

I left them reluctantly, and in a week, when I returned, I hastened to them as soon as I got out of the car. More flowers were there. They lasted only a day, but I had put in many bulbs, so there was a succession of oriental beauties. They had survived the snow, the weeks of frost, and the long burial in the ground, and perhaps just because they had endured so much they were strong and beautiful, with every bulb holding flowers. I liked them too because they came each morning, to give a new surprise of some strange colour and combination of shades in the one-day flowers. I try to describe them but I have no words for those golden-browns, those amber golds, those tiger-scarlets and sharp pinks and citron yellows and cyclamen oranges. The language of colour is muted. Colour is music, it has the range of musical notes, with sharps and chords and glissades, and only music can portray the colour of these flowers.

AUGUST

August is called the 'silent month', for bird song is subdued
and often absent, but the robin sings his little tune every
day on the edge of the bird bath, with an eye upon my
doings, and the dove calls 'Roo-oo-oo'. It is blessedly silent for
me because the gang of little boys have dispersed with their
Davy Crockett caps, their cracking pistols, their tin drums and
whistles and shrieks, and gone away to shout on the beaches of
Cornwall and Margate.

WISLEY

We drove to Wisley to see the gardens on one of the most
beautiful days in the world's galaxy of millions of days. It was
a morning of brilliant light and sunshine, a marvel of beauty,

166

which makes one astonished at this wealth of sky and earth. If we feel so intimately the sunlight and the atmospheric change, how much more must it affect the wild creatures, who sit in the sun and hide under the leaves, and feel the shafts of light upon their fur and feathers. A bird sunning itself on a bank, feathers spread out like a fan, may feel absolute bliss, and an ecstasy denied to mankind. Between animals and earth there is a bond which we seldom find, except on days like this.

We drove on this exquisite day through Windsor Great Park, a place for a tree-worshipper, and the great oaks, each a monument of fine growth and beauty of shape, stood alone, proud, magnificent individuals uncaring, while the cars swept past. I wonder whether these fine trees, so old, so rugged, have each their own name in the annals of the foresters who look after them. Each is of unique power and substance. So I gazed at recognised favourites, and nodded as we passed my own acquaintances, aloof and serene. I always think of Herne the Hunter's Oak in Windsor Park, and the lightning-blasted trees of Henry VIII's time.

We went through Sunningdale, Chobham, with its heather-clad common, and Byfleet, towns I do not know, but Wisley I have often visited to see the flowers at different times of the year. The roses were past their best, and the gladioli gardens had only buds, but we went first to the rock gardens, to see the gentians, the willow-gentians by the pools, the Farreri gentians, pale ice blue, the deep blue Macaulayi gentians. I can never see enough of these, I am avid for more and more. They lay in small pools of blue, but no other flower has the intensity of colour. They are jewel-like, cut from stone, ribbed, hard and brilliant and secretive in their power of enchantment. I first saw gentians growing wild on a hill in the Pyrenees, where we fought our way through the thick growth of cystus and spiny bushes, as we made a track for ourselves, across to a stream in the valley. Then, as we clambered down the rough rocks, I found these blue gems growing freely, and I picked a bunch to carry back to the little mountain inn. Gentians! I had never seen a picture, but somehow I knew these were the flowers of Paradise.

So we looked for the gentians at Wisley, artfully growing in little dells among streams, on screes of rock, in rocky shelters. We went to see the water lilies, blue and pink and white, and these blue lilies were new to me. Golden, amber, turquoise, azure, many flowers grew by the paths, and we walked among them, staring at them as if they were animals in a Zoo, captured for our content, yet always free and clear-eyed and innocent in a world far removed from their life.

'I don't like white roses,' said a petulant voice through a thicket of rose bushes, and the white roses cared nothing at all, but the words brought me back to earth with a shock, and took away immortality.

The yellowhammer chatters and chitters along the hedges, a companion who likes company, and this is a time for many birds to utter that homely chitter-chatter noise, a conversational style, reviewing the past season of sun and shower, of young broods and stealthy cats, and food and discovery. The swifts have gone, they were here and suddenly they are not here, screaming and crying as they hawk in the skies. It is lonely without those scimitar flights cutting the blue, making unknown curves of flight with never a collision as they dart, and I could lie out on the grass for hours watching them, trying to trace their paths. What are they doing all the time? Not feeding surely, for theirs is a fierce abandon to the golden air. They are celestial skaters on a great eternal pond of ice, each intent on his own pleasure, feeling the power of their wings, and the rush of air through their feathers. It is said they seldom come down to rest, they sleep in the air, and this is one of the mysteries of bird life. I saw more of them in Cheshire, where they were very abundant as they flew over my house. Here they come and go, and sometimes they are absent for a few days, until they disappear altogether on their long flight. In Cheshire I was always aware of them, they came each evening, till the end of their visit.

AUGUST

FOLK LORE

By the side of the road grow giant hemlocks, the kexies of country people, and some of these plants are six feet high. They bear white candelabra of flowers, which shine out in the darkness, and their green and spotted stems are hollow, so that we made whistles from them once upon a time. In Cheshire it was very unlucky to bring the kexies into the house, and several of the umbelliferae were debarred from entering our dwellings. These were called 'Mother-die', so there was no beating about the bush with regard to their fatal properties. My little Cheshire maid, Cynthia, was so upset when I brought some white flowers of the kex into the kitchen that she burst into tears. She implored me to throw them away. My mother or her mother would surely die very soon if I kept them. I threw them away, with reluctance, but I could not mock at her grief, and she was genuinely afraid. I had not heard of this saying before, but we never took hemlock into the house. We considered it a rough weed, which cattle would not eat. Their dry hollow stems were broken off and made many a game of shooting, whistling and drinking. This Cheshire girl never gathered the blue speedwell, for she said that a thunderstorm would follow. Her name, in general use among Cheshire country people, for this innocent flower was 'Thunderbolts'. My name is 'Bird's Eye'.

Little village boys never killed the beetles which slowly toiled through the grasses. They were afraid of causing a deluge, and the beetles were called 'Rain-beetles'. So the superstition saved their lives, as I wish a similar tradition would preserve bumble-bees from harm.

Dragon-flies were held in dread in Cheshire and Lancashire by children who called them 'edders', but I never saw these exquisite creatures until I was twelve years old. It was my great desire as a little girl to meet a dragon-fly and a dragon, a peacock and a peacock butterfly, a swan and a green woodpecker, a nightingale and a tiger-lily, but I only saw pictures of these

169

brilliant and fabulous things, which did not haunt our meadows and pastures.

There is a superstition about toads, which is held in many lands. The toad has venom in its head, say the old legends. The toad, when angered, spits out a poison which blinds the enemy. We liked toads, but we kept our distance and treated them as if they were very wise and very old and sacred. Once my son picked up a large toad which was walking on a road in France, and the French people cried out in horror. The peasants and the educated people were all perturbed. The animal had to be put down at once, there was such an uproar. They feared blindness, and hands had to be washed at once lest the poison adhered and eyes were touched.

I thought of Shakespeare's toad, which I met when I was very young and never forgot, for every child in the class knew about it. 'The toad, ugly and venomous, wears yet a precious jewel in his head,' we learned by heart.

My Scottie Macduff found a toad in the garden and began to play with it. He tried to roll it over and to pick it up before I could interfere with his games. Suddenly he yelped and flew round the garden, rolling in agony, and then rushing off madly. He would not allow me to get near, as he writhed and cried out. A white froth covered his mouth and I was not sure whether he was suddenly mad.

He was certainly poisoned, and he cried and moaned and rolled his head on the grass for a long time, while the toad sat, puffed up to twice its size, looking very cross. There seemed to be some froth on the toad too. When I could control the dog I washed his mouth which was much swollen, but the froth continued to pour from his lips, and it was several hours before he quietened. Since then he barks at toads but makes no effort to touch them and I hurry him away when one is in sight. The belief in a toad's poison is prevalent in Buckinghamshire, Cheshire and Derbyshire, and it may be in other counties. Yet we are pleased when a toad comes to live in the garden, we welcome it and try to keep it from harm, as it wanders slowly among the plants, or hides in the thick leaves of lilies and mint and pinks. It is like a tiny hump-backed man, a little old dwarf in a crinkled coat, a bewitched little gnome.

CHILTON

I have been again to a village I know well; partly to see the church and also to visit the great house of the village which was a school when I was there last. Chilton is one of the prettiest villages in Buckinghamshire; it has thatched cottages of the sixteenth and seventeenth centuries and a little thatched post office. The church is raised on a mound above the road. Its graveyard is like a green lawn with rose trees and flowers growing in it, and the path to the church has a wall of gravestones like ancient grey men standing there. There is a beautiful roof to the nave, Tudor work, and the chancel roof is fifteenth century. Between the chancel and the side chapel is a sixteenth century oak screen, and in the chapel there is a tomb to Sir John Croke (a knight wearing armour) and his wife. They lie there with the kneeling figures of their eight sons and three daughters below. There is a funeral helm hanging on a bracket high up on the chapel wall and on a wall in the nave is an hour-glass stand.

In the red-brick wall of the churchyard is a seventeenth century stone doorway which leads to Chilton House. This great house, the house of the Croke family, was rebuilt in 1740, on the site of an earlier house.

There are lawns and gardens here all surrounded by the old rosy walls upon which fruit trees grow. In the walls are small recesses, similar to those in the walls at Beaconsfield Rectory. The use of these cavities is not known, but it is supposed that they held little fires or some source of heat to keep the bricks warm in frosty weather and preserve fruit from the effects of frost.

The house is now a home for old people and it is one of the most beautiful and well-kept homes in the county. The dining-room has some of the original pictures hanging on the walls, and its great windows look down over a stretch of meadow and wood where hay-making was going on, and cattle were grazing. In one high room with panelled walls and polished floor, sat six old women round an oak table shelling peas for dinner; in another room a few men were listening to the wireless. An ancient woman tripped up the broad staircase with me to show me the bedroom where she slept with four others. It was a large high room with windows looking over the valley. Five little beds each with a quilt of patchwork stood in the room and bowls of peonies scented the air.

'We five are great friends. We go to bed at eight o'clock so that we can all talk together every night,' she said.

On the stairs a portrait of an exquisite lady of the eighteenth century, in pale green satin, gazed down at the stout little women in their sombre clothes, going about their small tasks. They were a very happy family of men and women in this house. They catch the bus and go out on adventure to see the films and markets. They go to church through the doorway in the old brick wall, so they only have to walk a short distance. They help in the garden, and help in the house, quietly and not too much.

I went over the kitchen garden, which was filled with vegetables and fruits, arranged in such a decorative design that it was like an embroidery within a frame, for the warden is a great gardener. There was a pattern and design about this garden, such as one seldom sees. The intersecting paths were bordered with pinks, as in little gardens long ago, and flowers had a place among the vegetables. I felt that I could be happy living in this home, with its tranquillity and kindness and understanding of the people's wants.

SPIDERS

A large cobweb beaded in silver hung on the fence this morning, August 25th, early, spread out like an intricate gauzy curtain with never a flaw in its design or workmanship. This cobweb is a thing of beauty, and I wish I could take a photograph of the radiating lines with the joining fibres, all set on the fence where the Virginia creeper grows. I have often tried to watch a spider spin a web, but my patience gives out. I think the spider is aware of my interest so she falls asleep till I go away. I have tried to see how those long bridges between two trees are made. These horizontal bridges appear miraculously, spanning a gap of a few feet, joining two trees which are near my garden door. It is said that the spider spins many lines as it drops vertically, and one can often see the spider apparently fall, with the line spinning out from the body. These lines are swung by the wind, and one of them may catch the twigs or leaves of the tree opposite. But the bridge is horizontal, and I see no crooked bridges such as would be found if the wind casually blew it to the tree. This is a curious piece of engineering, this swing bridge across a mighty chasm.

I recently met a woman who was really afraid of a spider. She would not stay in the room with one. She thinks they are evil. Is this revulsion common? Are country women as well as townswomen affected? I never heard of it before in my country childhood, where spiders were almost sacred.

'Never kill a spider,' they said, as they carried out the creatures in dusters or in hands and shook them to the air. It was the law of the land. 'It is unlucky to kill a spider,' said they. The tiny spiders which sometimes ran on our hands with minute legs tickling the sensitive skin, were called money-spiders. They brought good luck and lots of money. They were hailed with delight, for the fortune they brought with them. It might be only a sixpence found in the grass, or a gift of a penny from some kind friend, but it was the money-spider who had shown the way things were going. I am glad we looked after the spiders, and sent them out to the garden.

FIELD NAMES

Field names have a deep satisfaction, a mystery, and a

distinction, and the naming of fields is very old. Sometimes one may read these names in wills. Anthony Babington, in the late sixteenth century, mentioned some fields and they are still in a Derbyshire valley, Squirrels, Meadow Doles, Westwood and Hedge Grove. Our own fields were always called by their Christian names—White Field, Daisy Spot, Elliger Piece, Greeny Croft, Ley Oats, as our great grandfathers had called them, but we had no notion of the reasons for these titles. Was the biggest field called White Field because the wind rushed up continually, turning the mowing grass so that it was silver white? Was Greeny Croft so called because it was a convenient croft for the cattle, very green and sweet? Elliger Piece was something strangely named, a foreign sounding word, probably Elligo, and it was a mysterious field, with lovely hidden plants and springs. Daisy Spot was white with daisies, shining afar.

A very small croft, a wedge of grass between wood and lane in which a horse might be left for a day only, had the name of Forty Acre, a country joke which had been made a long time ago, and nobody smiled when it was used. Other more important little crofts had no names, they were not fields, but Forty Acre had kept its joke. There is the same country sarcasm, the sense of exaggeration in many a place name, and I have come across them here, where Hungry Hill, Poor Noll, Starveacre, Beggar's Piece and Littleworth Common carry names once used in contempt and laughter.

An old man who was born in this neighbourhood once told me the names of many of the fields, for he knew every one. Hilly Field and Copse Row Field by Long Bottom, and council houses were erected on Short-of-Mutton Meadow with Narrow Walls Field next to it, now occupied by shops. In Cheshire and in Derbyshire small fields were called Farthings, and perhaps the names of some houses may follow this tradition, for there are 'Farthings' around here. Some fields and woods are called after trees or animals. Alder Field, and Oak Field are common, Nut Acre and Briar Field, Gorsty Field, Badger Field, Squirrels, Kissing Wood and Lovers Wood, Shining

Wood, Bears Wood and Burgess Wood, Pretty Fields, Golden Meadow and Crazy Field (where buttercups grow).

Fields have been named after owners, after crops, after some old tradition, and sometimes with a feeling of poetry, as in Heaven's Below, the name of a great golden field. Poor un-yielding soil would give the title of Hungry Hill, which is a field near Coleshill, and there are other titles of poverty.

Local people are often not conscious of the implications of their field names and place names. They accept them because they have always heard them in daily use. So Old Dane, the name of a rolling field here, has probably nothing to do with the Danes, although I like to think it has. Hilly Field, Pegg's Fields, Copserows Field, Roundabout are some of the fields near me, and Stockings Farm Meadow, Well Meadow (with water) and Water-croft (with a spring).

I was charmed to see a sign-post pointing to Nettlebed and Christmas Common, when I first came to this part of the country. I expected to find Christmas trees growing on the common, with berried holly and mistletoe, and Nettlebed had a sinister sound for me. It is a pleasant little village, and the name is a reminder of the days when nettles were a good source of husbandry, for nettles were used in the manufacture of linen in the eighteenth century. We remember too that the Princess made nettle shirts for the eleven brothers turned into swans.

There is Egypt, a group of houses surrounded by woods, near the road to Windsor. The brook which runs through the hamlet is called the Nile—or is it the River Jordan? The names are used with country humour, but Egypt is called after the gypsies who came in the neighbourhood. Often one can see a couple of caravans, a tent, a few horses, a fire crackling and blazing, a line of washing out to dry on the hedge close to the signpost 'Egypt'.

Gibraltar is another curiously-named hamlet, tucked away in a corner, with an inn. The remoteness of Gibraltar seems to fit the tiny village. Probably the Gibraltar Inn was here first, and the place was called after it.

AUGUST

The names in Buckinghamshire have not the startling queerness of some of the country villages I know. Idridgehay, Whatstandwell, Kirk Ireton, Dove Holes, Hayfield and all the Dales, and localities Peep o' Day, Summer's Cross. Many of the villages had the word Ash in their names, for ash trees were plentiful, and we had Ashford, Ashover, Ashbourne and Ashley. I never heard of a street in my childhood, but everywhere there were lanes. Water Lane with its ponds; Dark Lane with its overhanging trees; Peg's Lane, Boggarty Lane where a boggart walked, Back Lane with Nicks and Jennels and narrow passages.

Buckinghamshire has musical words like Wing and Wendover, Whiteleaf and Penn, Maids Moreton and Ivinghoe, Princes Risborough and Lacey Green and the Scandinavian names Fingest and Skirmett. There are also a few odd names, Owlswick and Wardrobes.

SEPTEMBER

HEDGEHOGS

My son was startled the other night by loud noises at the back door of his cottage in North Buckinghamshire, a disturbance which appeared to be from some intruder who was drunkenly pushing his way about. He opened the door and there was nobody to be seen. In a minute the noise began again, and this time he found it was a hedgehog, which was huffing and grunting, scrabbling and rootling, like a man who is making up for lost time and grumbling all the while he works.

For the noise a hedgehog makes when he is really busy is astonishing. I have been alarmed myself at a racket in the middle of the night which must have been a hedgehog, although I have never been brave enough to go outside to discover him. In a ditch or under a hedge he scrabbles with his nose and feet

M

and grunts as if talking to himself, but at night, in the darkness, he lets himself go, and enjoys himself, especially if there is an empty tin or a dish. Early in the last war, in the silence of the night when we were expecting invasion at any time, the guard was turned out in my son's regiment because a hedgehog alarmed a sentry.

Hedgehogs travel at night, they explore and climb fences, and escape from captivity. They walk across the roads too, and many a time I see a little prickly corpse lying on the road, slain by a motorist. For neither his huffing nor his grunting can make the driver aware of his presence on a road which was his before man came to conquer. We had many friendly hedgehogs in my childhood, although everyone firmly believed the old superstition that hedgehogs drink milk from cows lying down. This has been seen by country people, who accept it as natural. We always looked after the small prickly little pigs with great interest. We gave them milk in a saucer on the lawn, and watched them drink at dusk. A friend of ours had a terrier which was a hedgehog hunter, and there were many skirmishes between 'Druin' and the round ball of a prickly hedgehog.

The Irish haymakers killed the hedgehogs they found in the fields, and roasted them for their dinners at night. Gypsies always ate roast hedgehog, saying it was like chicken. We felt it was an outlandish thing to do, like eating horse flesh, or frogs or snails, and only foreigners would enjoy such dishes.

Hedgehogs are supposed to hibernate in the winter but on January 7th this year I watched a hedgehog in the garden close to my window about four o'clock. It wandered up and down encircling the bird bath, sauntering along the edge of a flower border, then charging rapidly across the lawn and back again to the lily bed. When I moved a step it froze and remained immobile for a minute or two. Then on it went, nose to the ground, for half an hour, until at last it hurried off into the wood.

SEPTEMBER

STRAW DECORATIONS

As we drove to Burford on September 11th, for an autumnal visit to this Cotswold town which I love, we passed a farm whose hayricks clustered together, in the homely familiar way, making warmth and shelter. One stack had a beautiful cock made of straw perched on the ridge, not at the extreme end, but about a yard away, as if it had flown there. I was delighted to see this golden bird, for only once before, last December, I came across this intricate and clever work. This was at North Marston, on a haystack close to the side of the Oving road, and each year the stack has a fine ornament, made by a skilful thatcher. Once I entered a stackyard to look more closely at the ornamentation of the hayricks, and the farmer came out, wondering why I was there. He was surprised that anyone had troubled to visit his stacks, which he thatched and ornamented himself, and he was gratified that his work was admired. He had made the traditional rose and crown ornament for his stacks.

This is an old craft, which is in danger of disappearing, but now and then I come across a tassel of straw, a bunch of wheat ears spraying out like a bouquet on high, a clipped finial, a crown, decorating a haystack. The straw cock is a fine piece of work for it is suspended on wire in such a way that it swings round like a weathercock on the top of the stack.

We had a thatcher in my childhood, a man who lived in one of the upland hamlets, and I used to take the letter requesting him to come for the thatching. His cottage was in a bilberry wood, a fairytale place, and I picked the bilberries and stained my hands and mouth dark purple on my way home from the great adventure. This bearded man thatched the haystacks and cornricks and cottages for many a mile, and we had to wait sometimes for a few weeks before he was free to visit us.

The craft of thatching often descends from father to son, and in Buckinghamshire I know a family of thatchers famous for their smooth and beautiful work. The cottages are mostly covered with thatch in these little old Buckinghamshire villages, and even the small windows in the roofs have their neat, straw edge, and the porches over the doors have their thatch.

The thatcher takes with him twine neatly wound round a stick, or 'needle', some withybonds, and some spars or spicks for pegging them down. The spicks are made from young hazel twisted while green into hairpin shape. The thatcher has a knife for sharpening the spicks, a pair of shears for trimming the eaves, an oak bat for beating the thatch, and a comb made of wood for raking smooth the straw bundles. The end of this rake has a sharp point, which pierces holes for the spars to be put in. All of these tools are home-made, belonging to the thatcher.

In the Buckinghamshire cottages there is often a double strip of thatching along the ridge with ornamental edge clipped to a pattern. Along the eaves there is another pattern like herring-bone made by the lines of withy crossed between parallel lines. At the intersections of withies a spar is inserted. Many of the cottages have a wire netting to protect the thatch from birds.

Our haystacks were in the shape of houses, great oblong stacks with a ridged roof. The thatch was laid on so evenly and smoothly by the clever thatcher, it was a joy to see. We always went out to admire it, and to praise the man for his good work. At the corners the straw was drawn up to an ornamental tassel, which was cut off by the shears like a brush. Cornricks, which were conical, had a twist of straw with unthreshed ears at the summit. In Buckinghamshire the finial of a cornrick was called a rose and crown. It was made of four straw-plaits in loops round a centre stake, with a bunch of ears rising from the central stake. Sometimes the cornrick has a bunch of ears on the summit, spraying out like flowers. This ornamentation of the cornricks and the haystacks was a gesture of luxury, of pride and prosperity, but the luxury was that of earth's bounty, and the prosperity was the good harvest. This joy in making lovely things, in adding little extras for beauty's sake and not for use, is unfortunately disappearing in modern times.

PIPISTRELLE

We drove again to Dorchester Abbey on a day of early September when rain was in the air, and autumn mists filled the valleys. The great bare abbey was haunted, not by visible ghosts, but by an atmosphere of movement, as if the monks were walking the aisles and pacing the stone floor continuously, unheeding the visitors. I half expected to feel them brush past me, and the abbey was cold enough for many ghosts.

On one of the tombstones in the floor of the nave is an epitaph upon which I like to ponder, both for its good metaphor and for its terse poetry.

> Our life is nothing but a winter's day,
> Some only breake their fast and so away.
> Others stay longer and depart full fed
> The deepest age but sups and goes to bed.
> Hee's most in debt that lingers out the day.
> Who dies betimes has lesse and lesse to pay.

I stood there for a few minutes considering this comparison of an inn with life, and I thought of the arrival in 1684 of a coach from London or Oxford, and the bustle and noise in Dorchester at that time.

Then I was suddenly aware of a black rag near me, lying on the next tombstone, near my feet, a dark little rag which strangely moved as if animated by a breath, or by life itself. I was startled, and in a flash I thought of a dream I once had of a tiny black devil, caught in a tomb under a stone, and imprisoned there, released by a priest and then recaptured. I cried out and retreated in horror for a moment, and then gently we touched this thing with an outstretched toe. Such a squeaking and a shrieking arose, very high and harsh, as a very small pipistrelle bat struggled and flapped and beat its wings on the tombstone.

We inserted a thin postcard under the tiny creature, and raised it. It clung with its small claws like fingers to the edge of the card, its body and wings underneath, its little head and dark bright eyes peering over the rim at us in the most malignant way. It made no effort to fly, and it did not fall, but it clutched the thin card and ceased its wailing. It was a two-dimensional animal, like the small devil of my dream, but infinitely more pitiful. It seemed to be not of this world. We carried it slowly away from human danger, lest it should be trodden upon or taken captive, and we lowered it to the broken gargoyles and pieces of stonework in a corner. A few seconds afterwards we looked and it had completely disappeared in the darkness, back to its own secret life.

The broken gargoyles leered and smiled with their crooked lips, as if they knew all. The gargoyles on the roofs, the grotesques carved on the corbels in these old churches are in accord with the mediaeval spirit that made them, that conceived these beings; for the feeling of religion in the Middle Ages was different from our pious, reverent, hushed worship. It was allied to paganism; it was exciting, and wild, gay, cruel and scandalous, and these strange faces with leering mouths and half-shut eyes which fascinate me beyond measure, were life itself. The pipistrelle was part of this life. All creation was one, and this element of irreverent beings was a part, not shut off from God, but even entering the church to stay there for centuries.

Good Smells

Here are three good smells of childhood, which always give me pleasure. The smell of tar on a newly-made road. The smell of cow-cake in the great barn. The smell of resin (or 'rosin' as we called it) on the barks of the spruce trees in spring, when we rolled up the gummy, golden juices in our fingers. I must add a fourth, the delicious fragrance of a larch wood when the thin, green tassels appear.

his dolphin. The rhythm of the wind does not touch him in his timelessness, but his vitality is that of the trees behind him, he is lead, part of the living world as are they also.

This feeling for lead is born in me, as lead was born in Derbyshire hills. Not iron, or copper, not brass or silver, but lead was the metal which meant so much to country life. Pipes and taps were made of this soft malleable metal—not long pipes, for there were but short lengths to guide the water in its final path to stone trough and sink and sough. Boys scratched their initials on lead, and there were many ancient hieroglyphics cut there, like patterns on the silvery darkness, half under water. A lead pipe led to the cattle trough in the yard, and another to the horse trough, by the big apple tree and garden gate. The troughs were cut out of immense blocks of gritstone, from the hill quarries, and the lead had been mined in the neighbourhood up in the same hills. A small lead tap and pipe led the spring water to the drinking trough under the ferns, and another guided the water in the fields to its own sunken flower-embowered trough where the cows drank and children played and the birds sipped with delicate beaks.

SEPTEMBER BUNCH

Butter-and-eggs, with yellow butter and orange egg-yolks, a country name for toadflax, or wild snapdragon as children here call the flower: Robin's pincushion, the rose red protuberance which in spite of the prosaic explanation of an insect growth, still carries an atom of magic in its fine soft hairs, and its poetical name. Scarlet as minute pillar boxes the wild arum berries stand among the large green leaves in the hedges, and I gather one, with slimy stalk to add to my bunch, although many a fine Lord and Lady grows already in the unweeded corners of my garden. Then I came across a splendid company of wild flowers, on the hillside towards Whiteleaf, near Princes Risborough. Purple knapweed and blue scabious grew together, and these flowers were more beautiful than the ordinary ones.

SEPTEMBER

The knapweed was more delicate; the blue scabious, too, was smaller than the field scabious and of a rarer violet hue. In the evening light in that lonely place, with blue hills far away, the patch of flowers was beauty itself. In a field near grew blue chicory, with stalks of such toughness that one remembers the only way to pick the flowers is to strip off the pieces springing from the main stalk. I found crimson dogwood leaves, and pale pink elder leaves, and branches of hawthorn, just getting the first tinge of crimson, and some blue sloe berries. On the chalk grew the small clustered bell flower which is Dane's Blood, and hare-bells, while green and yellow crab apples hung from the crab apple trees and more bloomy sloes on the small stunted bushes.

At Tenby

At the end of the month I went to Tenby for a week's quiet rest by the pale gold sands, which stretch for miles, broken by rocky islets, and the long buttresses of layered and curved rock which hold back the sea. The hotel was perched on this rock, high above the waves, directly over them so that one could toss a stone down into the foam, and hear no sound when it fell. The continual roar of the water filled my ears day and night. I had not heard this sound for many years, for even in Cornwall I was farther from the sea's margin. In the night I leaned from my window to look for anything strange—a mermaid, a ship, a ghost—but all I saw was a line of naked footprints with no return. In the daytime I looked across the sea to Caldy Island where the prayers of the monks rise invisibly in thin spirals to God. The sea was too rough for me to sail across to the island, but I went there years ago, when the fuchsia hedges were in bloom.

The face of the rocky cliff upon which the small walled town is built, is hollowed with narrow caves, where we used to un-dress for bathing. As I walked along the deserted beach one morning when everyone had gone to lunch, I came across a sand castle made with care and artistry in front of one of the caves. At once I remembered a castle we made many years ago, in exactly the same place, such a fortification in sand that we could not bear to leave it for the waves to wash it away. Now I stopped to gaze at this castle whose architecture was unchanged through the years, with its six towers, its moat around it, and draw-bridge, made of thin strips of split driftwood, bound with twine, its turrets and inner ward, its gate-house and tunnels. It was a work of art. Later I passed by and the castle had been jumped upon and destroyed. *Sic transit.*

As soon as the tide went out far enough we went hunting for shells in the rock pools and by the island, in the rock crannies. Fans and cowries, razor shells and sea urchins, Chinese hats, and horns and cornets, Torbay bonnets and French hats, mermaid's purses and yellow corn, all were there, with purple shells and mother-of-pearl, and pink, amber and rose, and yellow shells. It is a fascinating pursuit this seeking for shells, holding them to the light, staring at the convolutes and spirals, tossing them back to the sea when a better specimen is found, storing them like a miser, peering at their beauty. A painting of shells always fascinates me, and in some of the Dutch seven-teenth century pictures beautiful shells are painted lying at the foot of bowls of flowers. Balthazar Van der Ast has many shells, and so has Ambrosius Bosschaert.

In one of my small Dutch flower paintings there are three pearly shells, one a murex, prickly as a porcupine, one a spiral and the third closed like a cowrie, all lying on a greenish table, where a fly crawls, below the rounded vase of tulips striped and prinked, the roses and lily-of-the-valley, the lavender iris and the fritillary.

A collection of shells seems to have as many colours as a bunch of flowers, as they glisten in the sea-water, and the pebbles of purple and green, of rose and pink granite are lovely as the sea anemones in the rock pools of quieter waters.

In the evening, just before dusk, when the tide was rushing in and breakers were foaming on the sands, fishermen appeared,

each with a rod and line, a bucket of bait and a tripod for holding the rod. They fish for bass or plaice, which come near the
shore, feeding where the waves break and turn up the sand to
disturb small creatures. Their bait is part of the mussel, fresh
from the rocks, or strips of clams dug up on the north shore or
razor fish. They throw the baited line into the sea to fall at the
white line of the breakers, and then they wait. One man had a
little bell attached to his rod, and the ringing of the bell when
the rod vibrated was the signal that a fish was biting. They had
good catches, sometimes seven or eight bass, and they went
home content, I think, except when a late swimmer floundered
around and disturbed the fish.

'It is a strange thing,' ruminated one of the fishermen, 'that
there are miles of deserted sands, but when a man comes to fish,
a woman must come round swimming in the same place;' and
gloomily we both watched a stout lady on a yellow surf board,
swimming near his three sharp hooks. She was not caught, but
the fish fled away.

TEAZEL

In the hedges we saw the juicy red berries of the guelder, and
the beautiful brown heads of teazel. I gathered a bunch and
took them home, for teazel is always strange and delightful to
me. Last spring I watched a teazel plant grow just outside my
gate, in the rough grass by the road. It grew with magical speed,
like Jack's beanstalk, spreading outward and upward until there
was a mighty plant with three score heads. As the green oval
heads got larger and the lavender blooms came to tinge them to
even greater beauty, the plant was like a candelabrum with
many purple candles. I feared somebody would notice it and
smash it, but it was untouched and it grew to its full splendour.
Then the flowers faded, and the seedboxes were left, for autumn
and winter decoration. The result of this is that teazel will come
up all over the garden, as once before happened, and lovely as it
is when wild, it is a pest when it grows with its strong tap-

root among the flowers. I like it, too, because it is a plant which was once used as the fuller's brush. The sharp curved prickles are much gentler in the 'teasing' of the wool than the metal brushes which are now used in machines.

OCTOBER

October is an exciting month, with no 'sere and yellow leaf', but an exhilaration in the air, a mystery, a deepening of earth's strength, so that one can feel the tug of the roots of trees, mighty beech and oak, and the roots of the rocks bracing against whatever may come. It is the prelude to autumn, the golden month, and for me this season is never melancholy, but filled with intense life and fire. The wind awakes and shakes back its hair and flings itself upon man and tree, in an age-long tussle. I stood at the window at the beginning of this month to watch the wind, which suddenly arose in a gust of great power. It seized a great chestnut tree in a rough orchard beyond my hedge; it shook the tree backward and forward, like a dog shaking a rat, and then, as the pendulum swung there was a crack and tearing sound, and a big branch of the tree crashed, torn off from the trunk. I rejoiced, for it was a tree which darkened my room, and caused me much tribulation through its density, and now sunshine can enter. The wind had done what a human being could not bring to pass. The sudden gale died away, the wind went on, gentle and mild. Its havoc was like that of a giant child, who plays and destroys and laughs and travels on.

October is the time when inspiration comes to artist and writer, to musician and to all who feel this inrush of the spirit of the earth, rising in autumn.

The stars glitter, as frost is in the air. The moon looks through one window in my long room, the setting sun glows through the opposite window, the moon on my right and the sun on my left, and this is something precious, a gift from heaven.

WINTER PREPARATIONS

October is the 'days-are-drawing-in' month, the preparer, when we take stock of fuel and radiators and firewood, and if possible we get in a load of logs ready for shortages. I look out for the log-woman who comes with her lorry-load each year, and begs an old skirt and a bunch of sage and a pair of shoes. 'It's the brown of the year, madam,' says she. I am glad I have some fallen branches lying in my little wood, for I still keep the tradition of providing for winter. I have an uneasy feeling that I ought to order candles and paraffin lest suddenly the electricity should fail, and coal should cease. Autumn has always been the month when we looked to our stores in outhouse and barn, in pantry and dairy and brewhouse, and the instinct for storage is very strong. Like a squirrel brought from the wild wood to captivity, I still look around for sources of heat and food.

Some apples hang on the trees, the late apples, but many have already gone to be spread on the floor of a bedroom. Pots of jam stand on the little larder shelf, diminutive jars for a very small house. There are no attics here to be stocked with apples, lying in neat rows on the wooden floors, as in my Cheshire house, no cellars to hold wood and homemade wine, and ghosts and spiders. I no longer grow the white stick of celery, which used to fill two long deep trenches in my home, for celery was something about which country people were very proud. 'Salary', they called it, or endearingly, 'Sally.'

In October our meals changed their substance, they had a richness and rareness of flavour which I try to recapture. Crisp white celery with a good heart, fresh from the garden, filled the tall old celery glass. The roots had been washed in spring water and scrubbed with a tiny brush, and a cluster of pale green leaves decorated each piece and a good white heart. There was a glitter about this celery, a flash of ice-cold water-drops from the depths of the rocks, and in the lamplight and candle-light it looked magical. Every house, every cottage grew its own celery and took pride in the ivory hearts, which are cut off and thrown away in the south of England. Freshly dug celery appeared each day, as a vegetable and for tea.

Roast apples also were October's fare, and every night there was a dish of apples, roasted to the exact pitch when the skin burst and the white foam of apple spilt out. 'A kiss' it was called. They were carried from the oven to the tea-table, and served with a large jug of thick cream, and a bowl of castor sugar. So I follow this tradition, for I grow the particular kind of apples with thin skin and pointed shape which make this delicate froth, and I have them for high tea. They were not served for any other meal, they were too delicate and too uncertain of their time of bursting.

A drink was made in the sixteenth century called 'Lamb's wool'. It was hot ale mixed with this foam of apple, spiced with cloves and cinnamon, and the taste was like cider. I should like to make this drink, snowy and frothing.

We used to have a posset at Christmas and on cold winter days, made of hot mulled ale, brown sugar and nutmeg, with spices and milk. It stood on the oven in the kitchen, in thick old mugs, and there was always laughter as people tasted it. The ale curdled the milk, and made a frothy surface, something like the Elizabethan 'Lamb's wool'. It was sometimes sipped from pewter tankards which stood on the high mantelpiece, when special guests were present in the kitchen.

Nuts are October's delicacy, and we pick the hazels in the woods here. We have to hunt for stones to crack them, in a stoneless country. In youth we had special smooth rocks which we remembered, with a handy stone or two near, and we left the tell-tale husks and shells lying in a heap, as if some squirrels had been there. This month I picked nuts from the borders of a cornfield, where a tractor was working, very late. Wild heartsease, yellow corn marigolds, corn camomile grew under the trees in the stubble, and above us waved the last red leaves of the wild cherry.

October is the month for roasting potatoes in their jackets. There was a square embroidered piece of linen with the words 'Roast Potatoes' in many colours in cross-stitch embroidered across the corner, and the hot roast potatoes were loosely folded in this, and placed in a large dish. We ate them with a teaspoon, not a knife and fork, and with them we had a pat of fresh butter, a jug of cream, and salt. We finished by eating the skin as a matter of course. Children chanted a rhyme:

> *Dearly beloved brethren, isn't it a sin,*
> *To eat roast potatoes and throw away the skin?*
> *The skin feeds pigs and the pigs feed you,*
> *Dearly beloved brethren—don't you think so too?*

So in October we eat this autumnal food.

AN OCTOBER DRIVE

October 12th. The sun was shining, after days of irresolution, so off we went in the early afternoon to catch some of the colour of autumn. We drove through High Wycombe, this once lovely town, now hiding its past beauty behind façades of multiple shops, and crowded pavements and packed roads where lorries laden with giant beech trunks, and lorries with loads of new cars, and lorries with straw and coal, and a circus with caravans and a fair with roundabouts, and all the cavalcade of this age pass slowly along the streets into the bottleneck and out again. As we stopped, caught in the traffic, we could see fine old doorways, the paint worn and faded, fanlights of the eighteenth century, glimpses of timbering down the alleys, all the reminders of other days.

We went through West Wycombe, with the lovely Swan Inn and the old houses, away to Fingest. We entered that haunting and lovely village from a high hill, slowly driving down among the beech woods, with the tower of Fingest church below, queer twin-turrets and all; then on to an unknown corner, bounded by more woods, turning gold and crimson and yellow. There is a parallelogram of country with Pishill and Stonor and Maidensgrove and Russells' Water, which is of great beauty.

Holly trees were scarlet with berries in the woods, and we wished them a 'Merry Christmas' and laughed at their fullness and beauty. Cherry trees hung their long crimson leaves, and the beeches bore some golden boughs among the green, for it is too early for the trees to change completely. Cobnuts in bunches of three or four, sloe, hawthorn aiges, rose hips, black bryony trails of scarlet berries, all hung in the lane, as we strolled with the dogs across pools of water and mud. We found some stones and cracked the cobnuts. We nibbled the aiges, we tasted the little sloes.

'Many Hips and Haws, Many Frosts and Snaws' says an old proverb, and this autumn presages a great snow and severe winter. The oaks are covered with acorns, so many that the trees are pale green, for the acorns seem to be as numerous as the leaves. 'October brings the acorn moon' is an old saying. Horse chestnuts have littered my yard from the overhanging trees, which are so heavily burdened with the polished brown nuts the branches dip down with the weight.

The beech mast smothers the roads, and I pick up handfuls

when nobody sees me, and crack the nuts and eat the sweet kernels. Cobnuts smother the little hazel trees in the lanes and woods, and we walk along, looking for stones to crack them. For some reason these nuts have to be eaten outside as one strolls along the paths, for if they are carried to the house and put on a dessert dish, they seem to shrink and fade and lose their beauty and magic. They are only 'nuts' instead of those enchanting things which were the source of a riddle, as we loitered home from school.

'Something you have never yet seen and will never see again,' we said, as we cracked a nut, held up the kernel and popped it into our mouth.

The aiges, from the hawthorns, are richer than ever, and the fleshy fruits are warm and mealy and floury as we taste and throw away the stones.

A heap of small fruit stones lies on my verandah, buried under a log of wood, and each round stone is perforated by a tiny hole, through which the kernel has been abstracted. What has done this with such neatness and precision? A mouse? The stones are hard, and I think they are the small stones of the wild cherry up in the wood, but the hoard is made with human delicacy, the stones touching one another, not spread out, but close-packed, dry, smooth and clean as ivory balls, hundreds of cherry stones.

Two Delights

Spindle berries are one of the lovely things of autumn, and in two days, October 21st and 22nd, I have seen two special sights for the gods. One a bush of spindle down the long lane which leads, most unromantically, past a sewerage bed, to a rough track with many flowers and berries. The spindle leaves are crimson and maroon and scarlet, with a fine green midrib, and never have I seen them more highly coloured, brighter even than the pink berries with gold centres which cluster on the twigs.

The second delight is a flock of gold crests twittering like the most excited happy little fairies, in a fir tree by my garden. Their cries are like those of some happy band of exploring immortals of minute size. Their feathers flash gold, and they move swiftly as they discover the seeds. Then, with no warning, they all depart.

On October 23rd there is a change, and leaves begin to fall in earnest. They drift down like flocks of birds, slowly, as if looking for a place to alight. At first I thought they really were birds settling down from the trees. They float over the lawn, each leaf perfect and composed to itself, as it flutters and beats invisible wings and twists in butterfly flight, before it composes its frail body on the grass. Then I see the bright yellow streak in the green of a woodpecker feeding with his back to me on the lawn among the green grasses and the yellow leaves, nearly camouflaged by the same colours.

GINGERBREAD MEN

Gingerbread men were made and sold in country places at Easter Fairs and Autumn Wakes, and they are still fashioned in the old moulds, for some were exhibited at the London Meeting of Women's Institutes. I have one of the prints for making these little figures, but mine dates from the time of the Napoleonic Wars. It is a solid block of wood, close-grained and hard, with seven designs cut and carved with intricate and delicate accuracy, four on one side and three on the back. There is a farmer with his sheaf of corn and sickle, an admiral with a shock of hair and a tricorne hat, a marine with sword, a little church with three windows and a tower, a bird on a tree, a basket of fruit and a sportsman. For perhaps a century it has not been used and today I took it to the house of some friends. I drove down a long rough lane in the fields, with holes and hillocks, and an open ploughfield on one side. In front of me moved a great tractor, and we crawled along until there was room for me to pass. It is always a hazardous adventure to bump along this narrow winding fieldway, where sometimes one meets a herd of cattle who refuse to go off the track.

In the kitchen there were three little children who were having a lesson in cookery. They had already made a pile of lilliputian cakes, iced in blue, green and pink, with 'hundreds and thousands' scattered on the tops. Sometimes they make minute loaves of bread or currant-eyed men, or scones as big as pennies. They weigh the ingredients, they mix with an electric mixer, they work deftly with no spills, and they fashion the cakes and drop them in the tins, ready for the oven. This is one of their delights when they pay a visit to their aunts and grandfather in the holidays. So these children, whose ages are eleven, seven and five, were charmed with the moulds for gingerbread men. They helped to press the fine gingerbread in the different shapes, they took off the thin layer with its stamped device, and then cut off the rough edges. Their aunt placed the tin with a dozen little figures in the oven and when they were baked we had them for elevenses. So again the finely carved mould is in use, and instead of hanging on the wall as an example of craftsmanship, it is back again doing its work.

In my childhood we had small moulds of block tin, with designs of a tree, a horse, and a leaf and a man, which I discovered in the dairy put away from former generations, and on baking day we were allowed to make pastry men, with currant eyes, or animals of dough, but there was nothing like this beautiful carved work. It might have been used for marzipan, the old marchpane, but gingerbread is its real use. The children were fascinated, as each small shape, with its sharp lines, was placed on the tin ready for baking.

We went to the sitting-room and dishes of tiny cakes were brought in, doll's tea-party food, all pretty and neat and well-cooked, little doughnuts as big as golf balls, the coloured cakes, light as air, and small as florins, and the plate of gingerbread men and animals and church and fruit. The three little cooks in their aprons carried them round, and their young aunts tasted and praised the fare. I thought this was a joyous game, which the little children will never forget.

A BEECH TREE

I have never lived so near a beech tree before. Over our farm-house hung a mighty elm, shallow-rooted on the rocky slope, but its roots must have wormed their way down into the great rock, and anchored themselves there, for in the wildest storms that swept over the hillside the elm was never weakened, it never dropped a bough or gave us alarm. It was at the back of the house, with its trunk behind the farm buildings, so we could not watch its changes except for the boughs that dipped over the back-kitchen roof into the yard. It dropped its green pennies in bunches in spring, and the cobbles were littered with bunches of soft fruits, which were swept away by the besom. In autumn it was a golden tree, and the leaves fell slowly down the roofs, fluttering lazily in the air for us to catch them. They dropped on the dog kennel, they painted the yard yellow-gold, they flew in at the attic window, and dropped on the floors of the little bedrooms. In winter we did not notice the elm tree, it faced the wind and fought its battles alone, for we also were fighting the wind, and had no spare emotion for a tree.

My beech tree in Buckinghamshire is always visible to me, and I see its perpetual changes from morning to night. Early each morning I draw back the curtains of my sitting-room and nod to it, to say good-day. It has a fresh aspect every time I see it, and I am aware of the myriad changes in rain and frost and sun. It is viewed each night as I draw the curtains across and ponder it standing there, where it has been two hundred years before this little house was built. Once it was on the edge of a wood, Burgess Wood, and there was a cornfield here, so my old Buckinghamshire friend told me.

In the spring its soft crinkled leaves will push out from the scales, and the golden scales will fall like rain, dropping with a sound of wind, and the pale gold tassels will hang there with the exquisite butterfly petals. These little tassels of flowers, these Victorian bobbles, will shake there, first on the low boughs then on the high ones, and the bees will fly among them, and the wild cherry tree by the side of the great beech will be rivalled in beauty.

There is a gentle sighing and movement in all the branches. The wood pigeons fly there and perch very high, and the rooks go up to the top of its steeple.

In summer, the tree is glorious with its myriad small leaves, its skirts of shaded green. Late in September one bough takes a golden colour, and the whole tree changes to red and amber, gold and tawny yellow, such a sight as enchants the spectator.

In October the winds fiercely attack and the air is filled with yellow rain, and flaming long branches which are loosened. It is supernatural, a maenad flying before a god, with the wind like the dogs of chase. One expects to see it drag up its roots and rush across a thousand miles of land and sea. It is a giant, a wonder.

The sun shines through the bare boughs and touches the ground, where now are thick carpets of the leaves. We brush up this fallen burden, we wheel it to a heap at the wood's end to make a leaf mould, but there is too much. We set fire to various small piles, making seven little bonfires in a row, and still the leaves fall. It is a continual wonder to see the number of leaves which fall from one great tree, and it would be easy enough to bury the Babes in the Wood, as I thought they were buried once, in our own beech trees, by robins carrying the golden and amber leaves in their small beaks. This story never filled me with alarm like Red Riding Hood. The babes were befriended and buried by robins, they lay warm under the leaves, as I so often did myself. It was a natural way of sleeping.

Then, the last leaf has gone and winter is here. The boughs are silver, they gleam like the little lead boy under their shade, the leaden child who is flecked with sunshine which now reaches him because the beech is bare and the light can touch his limbs. One morning there is snow, and I run quickly to draw the curtains to see my beloved tree, to see the whiteness on every bough and twig, a glittering and wonderful sight. The great lacy tree stands there, more beautiful than anything, an object to make the angels pause and stay on earth.

So the cycle goes on, and each and every day I see the tree for the first time on earth. It is a new vision. Nothing deadens its beauty, it is infinitely changeable.

NOVEMBER

Leaves are falling in their own sweet way; chestnut leaves drop heavily, spinning like tops with their five sails; sycamore falls with a thud like a dead body; beech leaves swing in the wind like millions of yellow butterflies, carried on layers of air, dropping, rising, choosing their resting place on the grass. Oak leaves drop lightly, slowly, solemnly, like brown rain. We try to catch a dancing leaf, for every leaf caught is a 'happy day', but how elusive they are, these fluttering alive things, which slip through the fingers and evade pursuit!

The pathway to the pillar box up the road is carpeted with the most intricate Persian carpet, citron and gold and copper, from the beech trees by the road. They spread their web over the ground until not an inch can be seen, and the oval coins make a pattern of gold for us to walk upon. Macduff trots on four dainty feet over this soft carpet, with lucky leaves tangled in his black hair, for a dog, being naturally lucky, can catch a leaf without any effort.

Cobnuts lie on the moss on the verges of the lanes; the hawthorn branches are dull crimson with the aiges or haws which cover them thickly; the rose hips flash scarlet; they have a strong reflecting surface, unlike the haws and sloes. Among these bushes the skeins of cobwebs hang like old knitting, damp and beaded with mists of autumn.

This is All Saints' Day, a day of ghosts and mists, of pale gold sunrays and azure skies, for there is a tradition of calm fine weather on All Saints, or All Hallows. Those born on November 1st never see ghosts, they are blessedly free from spectres. Yet I think I should not wish to be cut off from any vision of ghosts and goblins and spirits. November 2nd is All Souls' Day, when a reflection, a shadow, is part of life, when the souls can be seen flying upward, as mists and vapours—or is it imagination? The thrush sings a special song on the cherry tree by the garden, and the voice is so clear it is almost human. It sings softly, intimately, and then loudly, varying its notes at its will with obvious enjoyment and individual choice of musical sequence. The owls call in November, many of them in the woods here, warning of winter's approach, but there is nothing melancholic in the call. It is exciting, mysterious, eerie, and I go to answer it and receive an astonished reply. We always imitated bird calls, and tried our skill at question and answer, but with so many houses near, it is perhaps not respectable to hoot and call in the air, like owl or cuckoo or peewit.

THOR CAKE

I have been making traditional gingerbread cake, called in Derbyshire Thor or Thar cake, which was baked and eaten in the autumn for Guy Fawkes Day, and for the country Wakes Week when the swings and roundabouts came to the villages. It was a cake for the mid-morning, and slices were cut and eaten out of doors, with a mug of milk as we ran about. Here is the recipe, for it would be a pity if such a good and filling cake should disappear.

> 1 *lb. of medium oatmeal.*
> ½ *lb. of butter—and butter it should be.*
> ½ *lb. of demerara sugar.*
> 4 *oz. of black treacle.*
> ½ *oz. of ground ginger and a pinch of salt,*
> *mace and nutmeg.*
> 1 *egg.*
> 4 *oz. of sliced mixed candied peel.*

The dry ingredients are mixed, and the butter and warmed treacle added. The materials are kneaded together like bread, turned out on a pastry board and rolled in a piece about two inches thick. This is baked in a large greased and lined meat tin for about ¾ hour, until the cake is done. Slices are cut off as needed when the cake is cold. For tea it is eaten with butter. This used to be baked for our feast on Guy Fawkes Day, when we ate it out under the stars, with mugs of hot milk, and spiced elderberry wine.

There was a second baking in the spring, after Easter, when it fortified our spirits after the plain fare of Lent.

REMEMBRANCE SUNDAY

A misty grey morning after a night of heavy rain. I drove along wet roads with pools in the hollows, but the trees were hanging gold from the woods on both sides, branches meeting overhead in a long archway of colour, a tunnel of red-gold fire. The small grey church stood expectant in its leaf-strewn grave-yard, as people crowded in for Remembrance Sunday. Wreaths of poppies were carried up the aisle by a little old lady in a black felt hat who lives in a cottage near the church wicket gate, and by the Lord of the Manor who lives in the park. Side by side they bowed their heads at the altar, during the prayer of consecration.

NOVEMBER

We stood in silence for the long two minutes, thinking of the shades of that vast army travelling through the windswept sky, and the village boys among them. Then the Last Post and the Reveille were sounded by a young sailor and the notes of the bugle reverberated in the timbered roof and fell from the arches, startling us with the beauty and the poignancy. It seemed to be calling to the dead. 'Can you hear me? Can you hear me?' But never an answer rustled down from the myriad listening ones.

We sang our hymns and said our prayers, with one prayer which I have heard all my life, by household fires and in lonely houses.

'O Lord, support us all the day long of this troublous life until the shadows lengthen and the evening comes, and the busy world is hushed and the fever of life is over and our work done. Then, Lord, in Thy mercy, grant us a safe lodging, a holy rest, and peace at the last.'

The congregation drifted out to the little grassy triangle in the road, where the Cross of Remembrance stands by the ancient hollow trunk of an elm tree. Far away the distant hills and woods were blue in the mists. We stood in the soft pattering rain while the poppy wreaths were laid by the cross, and final prayers were said. Then a car roared along the road, breaking the quietness and peace, and the service was over for another year.

CHADDY POTS

Today, a frosty golden day of November, when fog fills the towns but in Buckinghamshire the lanes are coloured with red cherry, and pale gold maple, with rare bronze gold of beech, and yellow oak, with wisps of bryony wreathing the hedge tops, I went to Amersham, and talked to an old friend, a countryman who lives in an ancient low-ceilinged house, opening on to the road. He told me that the Dick pot, which was used by the women who made lace and those who did straw-plaiting, to keep themselves warm at their work, was called the Chaddy pot at

Amersham and Chesham. Names vary in different localities, and when a little town is lively, important and busy, it has its own independent name. These earthenware pots were filled with red-hot embers, and they rested on the floor close to the feet of the worker, as in Italy the women have charcoal vessels as they sit at market. I have never heard of these warmers being in use in the north of England, and we had none in our barns and outhouses where so many odd utensils were stored, but there was no lace-making or straw-plaiting in the cottage homes there.

In Buckinghamshire around Hyde Heath, there were many scores of workers who in living memory used to plait the delicate straw into its shapes for hatmaking or made the lovely pillow lace with its designs of water and flower and leaf, and these earthenware Dick pots or Chaddy pots were familiar objects in the homes.

They were a kind of central heating and a Chaddy pot created a good warmth to the feet.

ROADS

The ancient roads of England, the pack roads, the cattle tracks, the early British roads where the tribes of Iceni walked, the Roman roads, which sometimes took the same way as the British roads, all these are a fascination, and whenever I put a foot upon one of them I can see in imagination those people who once walked there and who may be there still, invisibly trudging along the grass ways on their bare feet.

The Lower and Upper Icknield Way are early British roads, which pass through Buckinghamshire, well known and mapped. They are marked with signposts, as if to show the ghosts of the early inhabitants of this country the way to go, and to see the words printed on the outstretched finger of the post—THE ICKNIELD WAY—is always a surprise. We get the same pleasure when we come across the signpost 'To the Roman Villa' in the Cotswolds.

We have been today along the Icknield Way, a favourite walk in autumn and spring. We turned down a narrow tree-hung lane, called Pixie's Lane, towards Bledlow Ridge, but at a triangle of grass in the middle of the roads we left the car and walked up the wild lane; the Icknield Way.

The grassy lane is broad, and the boundaries are high overgrown hedges of bushes and trees, which grow in luxuriance and beauty, as if they had taken from the soil some added richness and strength. Berries and fruits of every kind hang there, gleaming with colour, glittering in the sun, larger than on ordinary trees, and in the ancient days a lane like this must have been a source of food and drink, a harvest of fruit for the gathering.

We gathered boughs of sloe of such exquisite colour and bloom I felt sure I had never seen anything quite so beautiful. They were perfection, with the soft film of blue over the deeper blue of the plum, clustered together on the spiny black boughs, angular and sharp. There were scarlet hips from the roses which had blossomed in luxuriance, great sprays of wild roses which made trailing bunches of the rose hips. There was black bryony, and some delicate white bryony and guelder berries and dogwood and white beam and traveller's joy.

We picked deadly nightshade from a wood near, and gazed in strange fascination at the polished dark berries each in its green frill like a ruff round its neck. Five-pointed stars of green make these collars round the shining strongly-reflecting berries, the poison, the grief of animals, and our bane. I felt a superstitious fear as I held these fruits of the bella-donna.

So we dawdled up the steep grassy road between the delectable hedges, whose branches tossed against the sky hiding the view, but now and then a narrow gap allowed us to scramble through the broad hedge to peep at the distance, at hills and valleys below.

Every road, whether labelled the Icknield Way or a signposted main road, has its own individuality, and this applies to every road one has travelled upon. One way may induce the travellers to linger, to listen to birds, to gather flowers, another beckons to haste, it is sinister, and the haze has made it stealthy. It is unfriendly and cruelty is around the corner. Ghosts haunt some roads, and travellers speak of car lights which appear with no car, or accidents which happen for no reason, except the sudden appearance of a phantom. Fairies haunt some roads, fears haunt others, and joys are in a few irrespective of any personal memories of the journey's end, or the distant town to which the road leads.

The personality of each road perhaps depends on the use to which the road has been put, and the Icknield Way is tenanted by the unseen plodding shadows driving their cattle, walking softly under the overhanging wayfaring trees.

Once, near our Cheshire village, we were asked by a tramp on a country lane if the road led to London. It certainly led to London, and only a walk of three hundred miles lay ahead, but we did not mention this unimportant detail. This romantic way of regarding a road is one which a countryman often feels. All roads lead to London, to Scotland, to Rome. I look to the north and think I will walk for ever on that invisible way. I met a friend in London recently, as I was hurrying from Broadcasting House. 'Where are you going?' she asked. I told her. 'This is the wrong way. If you go straight on, you'll get to Scotland,' said she, so I turned about, for I had no time to walk to Scotland that day.

GYPSIES

A wild windy squally day with leaves tossing down, the last leaves left. My beech tree has its faded red-gold leaves in the lower boughs, and an oak in the garden wood is decked with fawn and shadowed leaves, but most have gone. In the morning a little call of birds—and long-tailed tits were there, playing in beech and oak, swinging, tossing, flirting their tails which seemed extraordinarily long. They were trapeze artistes, as they flew and danced on the branches, and their gaiety was infectious. I felt I was looking at pure happiness. An hour later they had disappeared.

We went off to the villages and woods of the Chilterns. Lunch at the 'Bull's Head' at Aylesbury, and the dining-room full as usual, baskets of flowers on the tables, waitresses ready. The owner in the doorway saw me, and came for a chat, as always. He told us about the people who have dinner parties there in the market town, the Free-Masons, the Ladies' Guilds, the Aylesbury Duck societies, the Turkey society, the Bowls, the Cricket, the Football, the Golf, the Hunt and the Farmers' Clubs.

Haddenham is always enclosed, secret and remote, disdainful of strangers and we drove round the wichert walls with their red-tiled roofs, seeking the church and the corner we knew. We went down 'No Through Roads' and turned back. We went round the curves, twisting and turning till we saw the church tower above a wall. I called at the house of acquaintances, but although I could see a group of ladies round the fire, nobody answered the bell. I felt I was a shadow from the dead, or rather that I was alive and these were shadows. So instead of rapping on the window I turned away and left them.

We drove along the narrow lanes, till we saw a red flag and warning of floods. So we turned back and cut across country, for rain was pouring down, and the roads were already half-covered with water through which we splashed. We were driving along the Port Way, a narrow lonely road, with grass verges and families of gypsies settled there. Perhaps this is a permanent resting-place off the track for these picturesque nomads who are moved on so relentlessly by law and order. The ancient road, Roman or perhaps British, is straight and narrow with broad verges and this same road goes through Oving, and appears in Berkshire.

The gypsies were a gaily-coloured crowd who sat round two big fires in the open, unheeding the pouring rain. Three caravans and some carts were drawn up on the grass, and a dozen horses, most of them piebald, were grazing in the thick herbage.

NOVEMBER

Children were playing, one of them was whittling something with his knife, others sat by one of the fires of sticks and brambles and brushwood, with the flames rising high in the air, colouring their cheeks scarlet with the heat. We were cold in our car, and we looked enviously at this bright scene of red and blue, gold and black, at dancing flame and crackling wood and sparks like stars.

Near this fire where the warmth was not too great, stood a large rocking-horse, a splendid toy, with flowing mane and tail and grey dappled body on two rockers. What a nursery for the horse, out under the sky, with these little ragged children to ride on its back! I blessed the kind people who had given this old favourite to these small children out in the wilds.

A gypsy sprang to his feet and stood with arms out, as if to warn us of the horses which were quietly feeding in this deserted road. Another fire burned near with older people around it and a large iron cooking pot suspended over it. Washing hung tattered and blowing on the wet hedge, and the gypsies sipped tea and stared at us. We passed them slowly, we waved our hands to them and they waved back. We left them with reluctance. No other car came along that Port Way, and as we splashed through these water-logged roads, we saw only two or three horse vans belonging to the Hunt on another grassy verge a mile or two away.

Then we found ourselves as drovers to a herd of cattle which walked very slowly in single file down the centre of a long narrow road. We crawled along, we stopped, we started again. There was no room to pass, and the cows strolled peacefully, some of them in-calf, not wishing to hurry, all of them mired up to their bellies from wet muddy fields and floods. For a long way we drove in low gear behind the cows, for when I see cattle in a road I become strongly protective, and I will not hasten these quiet-living animals. Nobody was behind to drive them, and we thought we were going to take them all the way to Aylesbury, as they solemnly plodded before us. There was no gateway, no farm, but only the Friesians, the Ayrshires, the

Short-horns and a Jersey cow and ourselves on this wet and ancient road, which seemed to be out of this modern time, in the past of fifty years ago.

Suddenly to our relief one of the animals turned aside into a hidden gateway, and they all followed, about five yards apart, twenty or more cows. There was the farm with its buildings, its stack-yards, and pointed conical stacks, its thatched barns, its orchard and its yard. There was a Rembrandt barn with ragged straw edges and dark interior. It was a secret and wonderful home, and the cattle had found it unaided, as cattle have always walked the fields and lanes, alone to their cowsheds.

I thought of our own procession of cows, which came from a distant field when somebody called to them from afar. Nobody led them, nobody drove them, we had only to open the gates and sing 'Coo-up' and they came.

When the cows were safely in the farmyard we sped across to Princes Risborough, with the white cross of Whiteleaf cut out on the chalk above us, but instead of continuing to the little town we went up the hills, and through the woods to a farm where I am always welcome. It was enchanting as ever. It was wet, and misty, it was golden and romantic. The trees were magnificent, oak and beech and a bare ash tree of great beauty, and a mighty chestnut. We walked down the drive lest the car should get bogged in the white slippery chalk, and we stepped past the russet thatched barn, with its open front, which is like the birthplace in Brueghel's "Adoration." It is the kind of barn in which Jesus was born, we thought, as we viewed the oak and stackwood, a saw and a feeding trough and manger.

We tapped on the back door, for that is the correct way to go to a farm, and we were welcomed into the whitewashed kitchen, with its stone sink and copper and pancheons, and beams, its steps down to a kind of shallow cellar.

We were taken to the house-room, to the big fire, where the fireplace is decked with the old horse brasses belonging to the house, and a curved settle with cushions makes a draughtproof retreat.

NOVEMBER

The old lady whom we called 'Auntie' was dead. She was a great walker, although over eighty. 'I shall die walking,' she had laughed a few days earlier. 'Hush! Don't say that! I'd rather die in my comfortable bed,' expostulated our friend, but the old lady set off for the bus, and quietly died by the side of the grassy lane. We picked up two countrywomen, standing, waiting for a lift. The rain drizzled and mizzled, the fog lay in the valley, but they were all smiles.

'It's a nice day for those who thinks it is,' said one of them cheerfully to me, and I decided inwardly that this was a good piece of philosophy.

Colour

We discussed colour the other night, its variation with the observer, the intensity of the sense at certain times, the value of colour in dress and surroundings, the physical effect of colour on human beings. A little modern house has had its plaster panels coloured pale pink, and the garden seats are pale yellow, and this colour juxtaposition gives me a feeling of sickness, which I cannot overcome or explain. It is the shade of yellow and the tone of the bluish pink that is intolerable, when seen both together.

In Jan Brueghel's pictures the artist uses a blue which makes the boundaries of space recede, and the tiny figures which one can scarcely see without a magnifying glass, are far away in this ultimate land, twenty miles or more distant. The people are wreathed in this blue aura, they live not only far away in space, but even in time. The inhabitants in the foregrounds are bright and clear, with a woman in a scarlet-red bodice, or a boy on horseback with a red jacket. There are no pinks or mauves or washed-out shades. The blues are in many notes of colour, which are only to be seen in the sky at certain times of light, after a storm or when the air is clear as crystal, or when snow crystals are sparkling in the cirrus clouds.

I saw such blue in the sky one late afternoon when rain had

poured down and ceased suddenly for half an hour for the sun
to beat through. Then came this celestial blue in the heavens.

FEATHER BEDS

I have been preparing for a visitor, airing a feather bed,
which was the best feather bed of my childhood from the parlour
bedroom. It has the clean sweet smell of feathers, soft as down.
This smell of a feather bed airing by a grand fire is something
one never forgets; it is a nostalgic smell, romantic and exciting
to the senses, with feathers and ticking and a faint damp odour.

I used to think it was more fragrant than roses and honeysuckle, because it carried so many promises and enchantments
with it. Perhaps somebody was coming to visit us, with pretty
clothes and perfume and books. Perhaps it meant Easter or
Christmas. It might be a children's party when everyone had to
stay the night. It was perhaps the visit of an aged Uncle with
tales of far-off days and presents of rose bushes and cough
drops. It might be a much-loved Canon who was coming to
stay for a week. We welcomed everything and everybody, and
the bed-airing was a forecast of things to come. Also it meant a
fire in an unused room, and I camped there and made it my
home, while the fire blazed in the polished grate and sparkled
on the brass fender, and the feather bed spread out its vast
bulk.

A bedroom fire was lighted about six o'clock. As I drove
home from school, up the long steep hill, I could see the gleam
of firelight from the window among the trees. There was a soft
glow behind the linen blinds and winter curtains, which warmed
my heart. I knew that I should be allowed to sit upstairs with a
candle on the carpet and do my homework on the bedroom
floor. That was indeed a great pleasure, far better than a table
and chair and lamp. Shadows would dance on the walls and
ceiling, everything would be transformed by an inner magic.

Chemistry and Physics would allure me with their beauties,
they would reveal some secrets of structure of the invisible, and

only Latin prose would stay resistant to candlelight on the floor and a feather bed airing.

So as I heap my feather bed before the electric fire, and pound the soft feathers, and shake up the thick thistle-down contents, I can smell this faint odour which brings instantaneously a vision of a bedroom by firelight, a candle on the floor, and books strewn over the carpet, while mahogany reflects the light and the religious pictures and texts on the walls seem to live and move of their own free will.

St. Andrew's Day

November 30th, St. Andrew's Day, called by the Buckinghamshire countryman, 'Tandra Day', and fog, mist, and grey shapes writhing about in the air, so that I feel cold and haunted as I look through the windows. Then I go outside, and all is changed, I am part of the strangeness, I am affected by the mystery of all these grey ghosts, whose movement is very exciting. The trees are marvellous against the grey background of mists, in the wood and by the side of the road. They appear and disappear, and take on a wavering motion as if they were enjoying a game of hide and seek. I share their happiness, and tomorrow will be December. St. Andrew's Day should always occur in a season of wet mists and watery shapes and slippery waves of water and air.

DECEMBER AGAIN

There are pleasures in going to London, such as one cannot get in any other great city, and I am always refreshed and stimulated by what I have seen. Even the arrival at Marylebone Station is something to treasure, with its smell of London, its misty gloom, its barrows of vegetables and flowers, cabbages or holly, sweet peas or cyclamen plants, according to the season, for there is a country atmosphere about Marylebone.

To look at pictures in the many little galleries is much better than to visit the great art galleries and one can enter into a little sketch by David Cox, a cloud scene by Constable, a crowd at a football match by Charles Cundall, or a very modern pattern of scarlet and lemon, which is like a band playing in the street.

DECEMBER AGAIN

A dealer may bring from an upper room a little picture by Jan Brueghel or Daniel Seghers, hidden away because everybody wants to buy it, and one gazes with misted eyes at the extreme beauty.

It is exciting to see horses in London, perhaps the Queen's horses in the Mall; I once saw riders in Regent Street; and it is a private joy to watch the flower-sellers, the man with his basket of pointed rosebuds in Regent Street, the woman with violets in Piccadilly. One can stand on Westminster Bridge and look down at the Thames, or loiter in Trafalgar Square among pigeons and 'lions' and children, or go to the markets which fill narrow streets with their clamour and bright fruit.

One sunless morning last April I wished to see the flowers at the Royal Horticultural Society, and I was driven along Piccadilly, across the wild stream of traffic at Hyde Park Corner, down Constitution Hill to Westminster, very fast, with the taxi driver chanting a long poem to me. It was called 'The Cloud, the Sun and the Persian' and he recited the complete poem as we flew along, for he wanted to share his own pleasure in the ballad. I enjoyed this drive with the philosopher who had the feelings of a poet. I had never heard of this poem which he had read in a magazine and liked so much he learned it.

A Christmas expedition to London is like a Christmas stocking filled with enthralling and personal gifts, some unexpected, like the book or doll's teaset at the top of the stocking, some expected but prized just the same, like the new shilling in the toe. The gifts in the London stocking are the shop windows, with their snow-white trees, and branches of frost and ice, the Fra Angelico angels in Liberty's, the mermaids and ballet girls which dance in the windows of a fairyland store. The unexpected occurs every minute, a smile, a joke, a recognition, a child's look, as one goes on a wandering, wavering way.

DOLLS' HOUSES

I had gone to London to see the exhibition of Dolls' Houses

in Park Lane, opened by Miss Yvonne Arnaud, smiling and gay, with her laughing golden voice, and her yellow roses. I looked through narrow curtained windows and into narrower doorways at the small interiors, with the odd feeling that I was an interloper in the world of small beings, and that these diminutive rooms belonged to lilliputians. There is the Longleat Dolls' House, made in 1870 for the three daughters of the fourth Marquess of Bath, a model of an Irish house which belonged to their grandfather. The house is neat, charming, complete, and astonishing. The roof is made of tiny oak shingles, in scallops like a petticoat edging in Victorian days, each shingle a separate scrap of carved wood. The eight rooms are furnished with exquisite care, so that one could linger for hours looking at the detail of furniture, china and familiar utensils. The kitchen with its range, its tap to the boiler, with its dresser and pots and copper pans; the drawing-room with bureau and blotter and books; the nursery with the cradle; bedrooms with hip baths; all contain the most delicious reminders of a family home. For me the best thing was the laundry with the iron boiler, and the diminutive flat irons, much smaller than 'The Flat Iron for a Farthing'; the wicker clothes-baskets, the piles of clean folded linen on the shelves, the towels with fringed ends hanging on a clothes-horse to air, the trivets and laundry table. In the hall, which leads to the staircase with a brass handrail, hangs a brown tweed coat, where the maid has placed it, and on the table are field glasses and the tray for cards. And then, when I had seen it all, I discovered under the stairs at the back, a cupboard with riding boots and shooting boots and a rifle and whip. It was complete and devastating in its perfection.

Another house, the Westbrook Baby House, was made in 1705 by the tradesmen of the Isle of Dogs for the small Elizabeth, daughter of John Westbrook, as a parting gift when the loved family left the district. It has been in the family ever since, and a white-haired old lady stood by it, the proud inheritor in these days. This solid and beautiful house, raised on a carved and turned stand, part of the original structure, is an evocative and haunting dwelling, something brought from another layer of time, trailing its own atmosphere of Queen Anne days, keeping its own air within the rooms, as no other piece of furniture or painting or work of art could evoke past days.

In the parlour is a needlework carpet, of gros-point, as fresh as if just embroidered. A flap-table of walnut has an inlay of light wood, laburnum or lime. There is a picture too small for me to distinguish, with a tortoiseshell frame. A silver candelabra hangs from the ceiling, a bit of Dutch workmanship, and of course all the candlesticks throughout the house are exquisite and touching, so that one gazes speechless, thinking of candlelight like the shine of the distant star, infinitely remote.

There is a chest of drawers with ivory knobs of fine workmanship and a bed with a high tester, with blue silk brocade valance, with blankets and mattress. As for the kitchen, it has a vast assembly of pipkins and saucepans, a spit, and a brass and steel grate. There are even tiny knives and two-pronged forks. In the hall on the table lies a three-cornered hat, for the small inhabitants of this Queen Anne house are men with wigs, brocade coats and knee-breeches. In a glass case in another part of the exhibition the silver 'toys' belonging to the house are shown, more candlesticks, plates and tea services, coffee pots, kettles, pans and pots fit for a fairy's use. Everything is in proportion here, but in some of the dolls' houses the collections of furniture are less admirable, even rather dusty and fusty, with the look of museum exhibits.

The kitchen is usually the most fascinating room in a dolls' house, and the most distinguished one I ever saw was in Bowes Museum, Yorkshire, where scores of copper saucepans, frying pans, fish kettles, pestle and mortar, and the well-known implements of the cook hang on the walls and adorn the shelves of a Dutch kitchen.

The tiny blue and white plates that stand on the dressers of these Baby Houses, the sauce boats and soup tureen, and square vegetable dishes are even more attractive than the furniture, and the knife boxes with horn-handled knives and tiny tin spoons or silver ones in the best houses, are a joy to see. If the dolls' house reflects the period when it was made, the small things within it are also models of the articles in domestic use at the time. There may be a spit and jack for roasting the meat, or a tinder box, or a warming-pan. A candle box is found in some of the houses, made of tin or brass, and this small object brought a response from my memory. In the pantry we had a cylindrical heavy tin box which hung on the whitewashed wall to hold wax candles. It was called a candle-bark, or perhaps a candle-barque, and this was its real name. Tallow candles and the home-made candles of my grandparents' time were hung by their wicks, twisted together, from the ceiling, out of the way of mice. Wax candles for bedrooms and for private use and not for farm lanterns, were kept snug in the candle-bark, which was refilled from packets on the high shelf.

Why is an exhibition like this so appealing? It is not nostalgic, for never had I seen such treasures in childhood, although perhaps they were imagined in reading some fairytale. It is deeper than memory, it is a vision of the inaccessible. We have an intense desire to touch each of these small treasures of silver, wood and bone, to try whether the lids fit, whether the taps turn, whether the minute tools will work. We are told that the very small plane in a model workshop, a little wooden plane about an inch long, will actually make curls of shavings. We are told that the brass keys turn in the locks, the bells ring, the doors open, but still we question.

Will the tiny teapot pour, and will the kettle boil? Will the milk jug hold a drop of milk, and will the drawers of the chests open smoothly? What is inside those leather trunks, those workbaskets and those corner cupboards? Tantalising they stand in place in the little rooms, and we shall never know, for our fingers are too clumsy to touch. We are certain that not only will the drawers slide open to display ravishing treasures of blue silk pelisses and cambric pantaloons frilled with lace and embroidered handkerchiefs, bonnets and ribbons and flounces, but rubies and pearls fill the jewel case, joiner's tools fill the carpenter's chest. The grates will burn with yellow flames of live fire, and the house will come to life when we are not there.

There is a 'Haunted House' with a grey ghost leering from a half-open closet, and a coffer at the foot of a four-poster bed spills gold coins to the floor. This house, in spite of its name and the obvious pretence of the supernatural, carries no sense of the macabre. It is matter-of-fact and dull, but other houses well-furnished and inhabited by respectable families of dolls are indeed haunted. I should not care to inspect them at midnight, when not only the houses might be lighted by spectral glow and vagrant flickers of glow-worm intensity, but revenants might appear *outside* the buildings, watching and listening to the movements within.

Do other people feel this queer half-sinister attraction in a dolls' house? It has been a component part of the whole picture for many years in my private view. It is the realisation that came with adolescence, when one looked at a dolls' house left from childhood play, with a vague realisation that something else was present, that life went on without the intervention of a human being, and one shut the door and walked quickly away.

So in the dimly lighted rooms of the exhibition I saw this hidden life waiting to continue, only interrupted by the women who peered and exclaimed and admired and sometimes shivered slightly as if a goose had walked over their grave.

One of my earliest recollections is of my dolls' house, which was so simple, so lacking in artistic merit, so poor in its architecture, it could never have appeared in even a village exhibition, but to me it was beautiful. It was contrived by my father from a stout sugar case which had held a hundredweight of lump sugar for household use. A partition was made across the middle, to form an upper and a lower room. It was planed smooth, and papered with a small patterned wallpaper, the bedroom blue, the downstairs pink, and ceilings and floors were covered with tiny rosebuds, like our own bedrooms.

The penny dolls, with china heads and smiling faces and little black painted boots on their minute feet, were installed with a few pieces of furniture from the village shop. A square table, a dresser, chairs with red silk seats, a bed with narrow lace flounce, and a lead fireplace. A miniature book with green cover, with the Kings and Queens of England, lay on the table, and a pair of ivory binoculars from somebody's bracelet rested on the dresser. Lead cups and saucers from 'Lucky Bags' and tin spoons from lemon kali boxes were the table ware. Plates were of rose petals, acorn cups were the ornaments. A cradle containing the baby doll, which cost a halfpenny, was made from a half walnut shell. A small dolls' mirror framed in gilt and a picture of Burns's cottage, both very old, hung on a wall.

This was my only doll's house, a dwelling remote from the Westbrook Baby House or the Longleat Dolls' House. Imagination is a grand furnisher, and it was perfection in my eyes.

DECEMBER EVENING

December 18th. It is four o'clock on this quiet afternoon, the yellow curtains are open, and a kind of magic lies over everything. We are waiting for a miracle, the earth and I, a miracle of night and stars. The wood is enchanted, transformed in this half-light. The naked trees, postured like a company of people of unearthly form or of primitive race, even people from Mars, grey-green, bent, swaying, alert, wait listening. They are intensely alive tonight, and they are revealed in themselves, so that we can see them. In front of them riding on his dolphin is the leaden boy, leaning over, aware of them, silver grey in this evening light. A robin sings a little hesitant trill. A white branch of an oak tree hangs over, ready to crash to the ground.

My fire blazes and crackles and explodes with sparks; it is a dangerous wild cat, burning the fir logs. The strange witchery of the wood and garden have invaded the house. The pink cyclamens, long beaks, long ears, listen and watch, and the porringer of freesias, lemon-coloured and lavender, my birthday present, scent the air. Groves of Roman hyacinths are in bloom, and these have been in flower since the first of November, a fragrant wood of white flowers in a Staffordshire bowl in which I used to wash my hands and face. The lights shine down on the pictures, the Dutch flower-piece of red and white old roses, and honeysuckle and Moses-in-the-bulrushes and fallen gooseberries, the river scene in ice-blue and green, the villagers at a ford. The copper bowl, which came from my grandfather's time, used in the farm for eggs, has lights on its sides. Parcels and letters and books, gilt paper and tissue and string lie on the table. The clock on the wall ticks loudly and wags its pendulum, 'O time, go slowly'. I sit here, waiting in this blissful quiet, with only the rustle of flames like autumn leaves, the thin chatter of sparks running with gold feet along the sooty roads of the chimney, and the insistent beat of time itself. Then the robin sings with sudden rapture in the darkness which is gathering about the house, its music a reminder of the magic out there. All experience has a truth revealed, and the smallest thing has a significance which was not realised in a stable balanced life.

Civilisation trembles on a knife-edge, the earth may be on the point of extinction in this century, but the beauty of the world is somehow enhanced through the realisation of the peril. Beauty of the invisible becomes visible in that dimension where we may wander without hurt and without hindrance. It is the essence of the unseen, the mystery of God and time and space; it quiets the mind as it reveals itself.

The carol singers are coming tonight, to stand in a half-circle in my long low room, to sing old religious songs.

> *God rest you merry, gentlemen,*
> *Let nothing you dismay.*
> *Remember Christ our Saviour*
> *Was born on Christmas Day.*
> *To save poor souls from Satan's power*
> *Which had long time gone astray,*

DECEMBER AGAIN

And it's tidings of comfort and joy,
Comfort and joy,
And it's tidings of comfort and joy.

Tomorrow will be a new day with all its freshness and secret unrolling of mystery, and Christmas is already stepping out from the sky.

3214